MASTERPIECES
OF
AMERICAN
GLASS

MASTERPIECES OF AMERICAN GLASS

The Corning Museum of Glass

The Toledo Museum of Art

Lillian Nassau Ltd.

Text by

Jane Shadel Spillman and Susanne K. Frantz

CROWN PUBLISHERS, INC. NEW YORK

Half title page. *"Amberina" was the first of the shaded art glasses that were immensely popular in the 1880s. See Page 42.*

Title page. *Mercury glass was patented by the New England Glass Company in 1855, but the firm had already exhibited "one large silver glass bowl on foot, richly engraved" at the New York Exhibition of 1853. See Page 45.*

Page vii. *In 1940, the Libbey Glass Company decided to produce a group of streamlined cut glass—the "Modern America" series. See Page 60.*

Page 1. *The national symbol, in widespread use after its adoption for the Great Seal of the United States, can be seen on this flask: the heraldic American eagle holding a thunderbolt, arrows, and an olive branch—symbols of war and peace—in its talons. See Page 28.*

Page 3. *This flask depicts a horse-drawn cart that runs on iron rails. See Page 29.*

Copyright © 1990 by The Corning Museum of Glass

Published by Crown Publishers, Inc., 201 East 50th Street, New York, New York 10022

CROWN is a trademark of Crown Publishers, Inc.

Manufactured in Japan

Library of Congress Cataloging-in-Publication Data
Spillman, Jane Shadel.
Masterpieces of American glass : the Corning Museum of Glass and the Toledo Museum of Art and Lillian Nassau Ltd. / by Jane Shadel Spillman and Susanne K. Frantz.
p. cm.
Catalog of an exhibition held at Steuben Glass, January 30, 1990–February 25, 1990 and in Moscow, April 1990.
1. Glassware—United States—Exhibitions. 2. Corning Museum of Glass—Exhibitions. 3. Toledo Museum of Art—Exhibitions. I. Frantz, Susanne K. II. Corning Museum of Glass. III. Toledo Museum of Art. IV. Steuben Glass, Inc. V. Title.
NK5112.S67 1990
748.2913′074′47312—dc20 89–10000
ISBN 0-517-57324-5

Book design by June Marie Bennett

10 9 8 7 6 5 4 3 2 1

First Edition

Contents

Foreword

Glassmaking was America's first industry. It began here early in the 17th century with the arrival of European colonists on the Atlantic coast. Raw materials were available in abundance, and it was difficult and expensive to ship fragile glass to the growing population.

The products of the American glasshouses built for the next 200 years were essentially imitations of European wares. Most of the workers were trained in Europe, and most of their customers were European either by birth or by outlook. There was one significant difference, however. Many European glass factories were financed by wealthy noble families, and their products were destined for the tables of the rich. These lavish products have no parallel in America's glassmaking history. In colonial America, the owners of glasshouses were merchant-entrepreneurs who thought that they could make money producing humble table and storage wares and window glass, and that they could undersell imported products. The wealthy tended to import more elaborate glassware from abroad.

Dozens of factories were started, but most failed quickly due to mismanagement and the pressure of foreign competition. It was not until the second quarter of the 19th century that American glassmakers achieved financial security through the development of methods for mass-producing bottles and table glass at greatly reduced cost. Suddenly, everyone could afford decorative glass, and it was widely available.

At the end of the 19th century, glass factories were operating throughout the United States. American inventors led the world in developing faster and faster methods for producing glass objects, but our achievements were not limited to advances in mass production. Around 1900, the American glassmaker Louis Comfort Tiffany became famous in Europe for his work related to the Art Nouveau style. Later, several other factories also achieved world renown for their production of decorative, nonfunctional wares. Two of the firms (whose products are included here) were Steuben Glass and the Libbey Glass Company.

Until the late 1950s, nearly everything made of glass was functional. Our glassmaking history then entered a dramatic new phase as artists began to use glass to create art. Since that time, hundreds, perhaps thousands, of artists and craftsmen have studied this intriguing material. Today they are producing artistic works that transcend glass's utilitarian beginnings.

The objects illustrated here document America's glassmaking history. We have chosen the most beautiful and historically important examples from two of the most comprehensive collections in the world. These collections belong to The Corning Museum of Glass and The Toledo Museum of Art, each of which is located in an important American glassmaking center. In addition, we have selected a Tiffany lamp from the leading American dealer specializing in Art Nouveau glass.

We believe that understanding the glassmaking history of the United States gives clear insights into who we are as a people and why our country developed as it did in the nearly 400 years since the first European colonists arrived here. We hope that the citizens of the Soviet Union, to whom this exhibition will be traveling, will enjoy learning about us through seeing these treasures of American glass.

Dwight P. Lanmon, Director
The Corning Museum of Glass

Roger Mandle, former Director
The Toledo Museum of Art

1

The Beginning

Christopher Columbus discovered the New World in 1492. Exploration continued throughout the following century, but there were no permanent colonies in North America until the 17th century, and no English colonies until after 1600. The earliest glass factories in the Americas were in Mexico (founded in 1535 by the first governor of New Spain) and in Argentina (run by Venetians in 1592). Neither flourished, however, for the Spanish never actively promoted manufacturing in their New World possessions. Also, as the European populations of the Spanish (and, later, French) colonies were never very large, there was not as strong a demand for glass as that which existed in the more populous English settlements. Thus, the story of American glassmaking concerns the British and Dutch colonies exclusively; except for the one factory in Mexico, glass was not made in the French or Spanish colonies in North America.

The first permanent English settlement in the Western Hemisphere was at Jamestown in the colony of Virginia. It was founded and governed by a group of merchant investors trading as the London Company of Virginia. Living conditions were primitive during the first few years, and most of the original group of colonists soon died, but the settlement eventually grew into a thriving and prosperous colony, with tobacco and lumber as its chief exports in the 17th century.

The colony of Virginia was founded principally to furnish English manufacturers with raw materials, but the merchant investors who made up the London Company were also alert for profitable manufactures that could be carried on there. One obvious choice was glassmaking. The area was heavily wooded, so fuel for the furnaces—in short supply in England—was abundant, and it was assumed that the raw materials necessary for glassmaking could be found nearby. At the beginning of the 18th century, the demand for window and table glass had increased greatly, and the factories in England could not supply the market. Table glass was being imported from Venice at high cost, and the investors in London must have thought it would be cheaper and more profitable to make glass in Virginia than to bring it in from the Adriatic.

The first colonists arrived in Jamestown in 1607, and when the ship's captain, Christopher Newport, returned to England, he assured the backers that the necessary raw materials for making glass were there.

When Newport arrived again in 1608, he brought 70 settlers, among them 8 Polish and German artisans especially recruited to set up and run a glasshouse in the colony. (Other settlers were to manufacture soap, pitch, tar, clapboards, wainscoting, and other products.) John Smith, the colony's military leader, records that the factory was built in the woods, about a mile from the settlement. When Newport left for England later that year, he took with him samples of the craftsmen's work, including glass. Exactly what the glass objects were is not recorded, but it is likely that they included bottles or windowpanes; it is unlikely that tableware or beads were being produced. Glass was also made in the spring of 1609, but it is probable that the venture ended when Smith returned to England in the fall of that year. During the following winter, known as the "starving time," 550 of the 610 colonists died, including all of the glassmakers.

The London Company tried a dozen years later to reintroduce the manufacturing of glass. This time, an investor named William Norton set up a stock company to finance the venture and sailed for Virginia with his wife and children, several servants, and six Italian glassmakers and their families. Norton's intention was to make all types of glass and beads, the latter presumably for trade with the Indians. This glasshouse fared no better than the first one. The furnace cracked, the glassblowers quarreled among themselves, Captain Norton died, and the venture was finally given up when the Virginia colony came under the direct control of the Crown in 1624. Despite these failures, glassmaking can be said to have been America's first industry—the first manufacturing enterprise started in the English colonies of the New World.

The need for glass in the American colonies was so great that, in spite of such obvious difficulties as the distance from London and the lack of experienced glassmakers, colonists tried to produce it again and again. Massachusetts Bay colonists started a glasshouse in Salem, north of Boston, in 1641. Another factory was planned at Philadelphia in 1682, and Dutch colonists in New Amsterdam (later renamed New York) operated two glasshouses in the 1650s. What these glasshouses produced is not known. None operated for more than a few years, and no identified products have survived.

Most of the time, American colonists relied on imported glassware—or did without. As early as 1687, Samuel Sewall recorded in his diary that "Mr. Mather had two Venice glasses broken at our meeting." If Cotton Mather, the famous Puritan clergyman, had Venetian wineglasses in his cupboard, it is probable that other well-to-do colonists had them as well. Similar references can be found for the use of Venetian glass in the Virginia colony in the 17th century. The Dutch settlers in New Amsterdam and Fort Orange (present-day Albany) used elaborate Dutch wineglasses, but these glasses were probably unusual and very costly. Less prosperous settlers used wooden and pewter drinking vessels.

Francis Higginson, who wrote a book of advice for prospective colonists in 1629, said, "Be sure to furnish yourself with glass for windows." Settlers who could afford to do so brought them from England. Window glass was such a scarce commodity in the 17th century that windows were sometimes stolen.

Numerous merchants advertised imported glassware in newspapers throughout the 18th century. George Washington ordered glass from England for

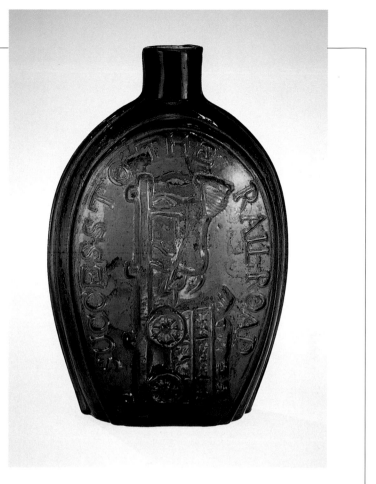

use at Mount Vernon, his Virginia plantation. From 1757 to 1773, he ordered 1,200 panes of window glass, 23 dozen pieces of stemware, 16 decanters, 6 milk pots, 12 dozen porter bottles, a number of garden bells (for protecting tender seedlings and speeding their growth), and an assortment of other glassware for the table. Although he could have purchased the glass in nearby Williamsburg or Alexandria, he thought that he could get better quality at less expense by ordering directly from merchants in England. English glass was readily available to the colonists in or near cities, but it was costly. This circumstance was a considerable impetus to the American glass industry.

2

18th-Century Factories

1. Bottles and windows were the staple products of the American glass industry until the end of the 19th century. This bottle's form is similar to that current in northern Europe in the mid-18th century. According to family tradition, it was made for Richard Wistar, eldest son of Caspar Wistar, the founder of the Wistarburgh Glassworks, which was situated near Alloway, New Jersey, c. 1745–1755. This and two other bottles with identifiable Philadelphia owners' initials are all that can be identified of the thousands of bottles produced for 37 years at the Wistar factory.

It was not until the 18th century that commercially successful glass factories were started in North America, although there was certainly a large market for window and bottle glass. One contemporary writer in the *Maryland Gazette* commented on the need for a bottle glass manufactory to supply the brewers of beer and porter with containers. The large tracts of forest, which were a hindrance to agriculture, were also an encouragement to glassmaking. Glassmaking (unlike cabinetmaking, silversmithing, and other crafts that supplied the colonial populace with goods) required, at minimum, a few experienced workmen, one person with experience in mixing the glass batch and

2. It is difficult to attribute many glass objects to specific American glasshouses or even to say with certainty that they were made in the United States. The form and decoration of this mug, c. 1760–1810, have close parallels in Spain and Germany, but its proportions are most closely related to a group of glass vessels found in America and presumably made there. In addition, the ribbed strapwork handle strongly resembles the handles on pitchers and mugs associated with New Jersey glasshouses. A related mug was found in excavations of Benjamin Franklin's house in Philadelphia. Franklin purchased glass tubes for conducting electrical experiments from Caspar Wistar, and he may have bought that mug from him, too.

with knowledge of furnace construction, and a considerable amount of raw material and fuel before any salable products could be made. These requirements made a substantial capital outlay a necessity for any would-be glassmaker, and they explain why other crafts flourished in the Colonies well before glassmaking did.

Nearly 20 glass factories were started between 1732 and 1780. The three most important ones were founded by Germans, but surprisingly two of the three managers or owners had no prior experience with glassmaking. Most of the workers were Germans as well, for investors found it easier to induce German rather than English glassblowers to come to the New World. The German economy was less stable in the 18th century because of a lack of unity among the German states, and many glassblowers were out of work. Traditionally, glassblowers were itinerant laborers anyway, so with a guarantee of employment it was easier to persuade them to emigrate. In England, where the glass industry was flourishing, full employment removed an important reason for glassblowers to leave. Moreover, English mercantile policies forbade their emigration.

3. This candlestick, c. 1739–1776, is attributed to the Wistar glasshouse, near Alloway, N.J., on the basis of two blue glass tapersticks of similar form, documented as having descended in the Wistar family. While blue glass is known to have been made at the Wistarburgh factory, amethyst glass is not. However, since colorless glass is also thought to have been made at the factory, the decolorant manganese oxide was almost certainly used. By adding a small amount more of manganese oxide, the purple color could have been produced.

A glasshouse near Alloway in Salem County, New Jersey, south of Philadelphia, was the first successful glass factory in the English colonies of North America. Its founder, Caspar Wistar, came to Philadelphia from the Rhineland in 1717, when he was only 20. His training was as a huntsman. He learned the trade of brass button making in Philadelphia, married into that city's Quaker society, and in only a few years was a prosperous merchant retailing brass buttons as well as many kinds of German-made goods in his own store. Exactly why Wistar decided to invest in a glass factory is not known, but since he seems to have been a shrewd businessman, he must have thought that his factory would be able to undersell imported glassware. In 1738, he signed a contract with four German glassblowers and financed the building of a glasshouse on land he had bought in southern New Jersey. By the following year, the glasshouse at Wistarburgh was in production, using wood from nearby forests for fuel and local sand and wood ashes (to make potash) as the principal raw materials. It was probably the availability of the large

tracts of woodland that prompted the location in New Jersey rather than in Pennsylvania, where much of the land near Philadelphia had already been cleared for farming. The glass formula was typical *Waldglas* or forest glass, an impure greenish glass common throughout northern Europe since the Middle Ages.

Wistar's advertisements indicate that he produced mainly window glass and bottles, the two glass products most needed in the Colonies. The largest volume of his output was green glass bottles (figure 1), which were in great demand among the colonists. More than 15,000 bottles were produced in a typical year. Liquor bottles, case bottles, vials, and chemical glassware were among the products of the factory. Because Wistar's bottles looked just like bottles made in northern Europe, there is no way to distinguish undocumented ones from Continental bottles, which were plentiful in the Colonies.

Electrical ("electerising") apparatus was mentioned in an advertisement, and was presumably the sort used by Benjamin Franklin and others in their experiments with electricity. The rubbing of glass tubes to generate static electricity fascinated scientists on both sides of the Atlantic. Eventually, Franklin's interest brought him international acclaim when he proved that lightning is a form of electricity.

Tableware was also produced at the Wistar factory, but it was not marked, so it is difficult to identify today. Some green sugar bowls with ribbed and/or applied decoration are thought to have been made there. Several cylindrical green mugs with horizontal threading (figure 2) have been attributed to the factory as well; one of these mugs was found during archeological excavations at the site of Benjamin Franklin's house, and he is known to have been a customer of Wistar's store, which was only a few blocks away. Colorless and blue tableware has also been associated with the factory, and purple glass (figure 3) may have been made there.

The making of glass was officially discouraged by the British authorities, who viewed the Colonies as producing only raw materials for British manufacturers. In the mid-18th century, however, there was considerable interest in the manufacture of glass in several colonies, particularly Massachusetts, New York, and Pennsylvania. When the English government levied duties on imported glassware in 1767, new impetus was given to local manufactures. Thus, although Caspar Wistar had died in 1752, his son, Richard, managed the factory until it closed about 1776.

Among the pre–Revolutionary War factories in the Colonies, the most famous today are those of Henry William Stiegel, who operated two or three separate glasshouses during his very brief career in the industry. Stiegel came from Germany to Philadelphia in 1750, and he soon found employment with an ironmaster in Lancaster County, a center of German settlement west of Philadelphia. Stiegel married the ironmaster's daughter and became a partner in the ironworks. He manufactured cast-iron stove plates, and he and several partners soon began to invest in land. In 1763, Stiegel opened his first glasshouse, probably for manufacturing bottles and window glass. Among his blowers was Christian Nasel, who had worked at the Wistar factory for 12 years or more. The other workmen were also of German descent, and it is likely that Stiegel's output in this glasshouse was similar to the wares made at

5. There are precedents in Europe for much American 18th-century glass. This sugar bowl, c. 1769–1774, has close parallels in England. While no surviving examples are documented as products of the factories owned by Henry William Stiegel, his glassworks is a likely source. Stiegel's was the only American factory known to have produced lead glass before the Revolutionary War, when such objects as this sugar bowl would have been fashionable.

Wistarburgh. Governor Penn of Pennsylvania described it in 1767 as "of very ordinary Quality . . . to supply the small demands of the Villages and Farmers in the adjacent inland Country."

Presumably this factory was a financial success because, within a few years, Stiegel built a second glasshouse, this time at Manheim, a community he helped found in Lancaster County. He closed the first factory and moved the blowers to Manheim, where they continued to make the same products. However, at the American Flint Glass Manufactory, as he called the new glasshouse, Stiegel was determined to produce fine lead-glass tableware in the English tradition. He is believed to have made a trip to England in 1763 to recruit blowers, and by 1769 he

is said to have built a third glasshouse. At that time, he was advertising an extensive assortment of "white and blue flint" (or lead) glass tableware, including tumblers and decanters in several sizes, water bottles, wine and water glasses, serving glasses for salt and cream, cruets for vinegar and mustard, and vials for chemists and apothecaries. Factory records also show the production of thousands of pocket bottles (figure 4). His factory prospered for several years, but his continued expansion led to more debt than he could manage. By 1774, he was nearing bankruptcy, and he was forced to close the glasshouse. Thus, Stiegel's career as a glassmaker was much shorter than Wistar's—only 11 years in all.

There is considerable disagreement about exactly what Stiegel produced and for whom. Logically, one might suppose that he would have supplied his German neighbors with the sort of glassware they had had at home. From 1763 until 1768 or 1769, his principal products may have included Germanic shapes. This local market was very limited, however, and when he began to manufacture lead glass, it was almost certainly in the English style (figure 5). Stiegel advertised his products in New York, Boston,

6. The identity of G. F. Mauerhoff has eluded scholars. This goblet bearing his name was found in Europe. The inscription on the reverse, "New Bremen, State of Maryland. Frederik County. 1792," suggests that the recipient of this goblet may not have been familiar with American geography or the location of the New Bremen Glassmanufactory. This goblet was probably a gift to one of the German investors who helped finance the factory. The engraving, among the finest known on Amelung's glass, includes both matte and polished details. Originally, the goblet probably had a domed cover, with the finial matching the form of the baluster knop in the stem. Goblets of the same form and with engraved decoration in similar Rococo style were also produced in Germany in the late 18th century.

7. This beaker was made for George and Metha Repold. Repold was an influential merchant with whom Amelung dealt in Baltimore, Maryland. Six glasses that belonged to the Repold family have been attributed to Amelung's factory. One, apparently a gift from Amelung's wife, is dated 1792.

8. Bottles in this color and with "broken swirl" ribbing are known today as "Pitkin" type. One glasshouse, located at East Hartford, Connecticut, and owned by the Pitkin family, is known to have made such objects, but at least four factories along the Eastern Seaboard of the United States produced similar bottles, c. 1790–1810.

Philadelphia, and Baltimore, as well as in newspapers in Virginia and South Carolina.

In 1771, Stiegel advertised for a "cutter and flowerer." For about a year, from June 1773 until mid-1774, he employed Lazarus Isaacs, an English glass engraver. Isaacs had emigrated to Philadelphia and advertised his services as an independent engraver decorating glass with "coats of arms, flowers, names or figures." This gives an idea of what he may have been engraving when he worked for Stiegel. To date, only one engraved piece, a goblet commemorating his daughter's marriage, has been attributed to Stiegel.

Stiegel's effort to produce English-style glassware and to compete directly with imported wares was the first attempt by a colonial glassmaker to enter the market for luxury products. Unfortunately, his appeals to the "buy American" patriotism of his customers did not win him sufficient patronage to stave off bankruptcy.

Stiegel's fame today rests primarily on the romantic and fascinating stories surrounding his life. He represents a popular American "rags to riches" story. He arrived with very few possessions, but he soon became an ironmaster, built two mansions and two or three glasshouses, founded the town of Manheim (providing the land for the Lutheran church there and requesting as annual rental only one red rose in perpetuity), and lived so lavishly that his neighbors called him "Baron." He died in poverty around 1780, having lost both his iron and glass businesses to creditors.

9. *Small bowls such as this were probably intended for punch, though it is likely that this bowl held enough for only one or two people. The form is closely related in shape and size to ceramic punch bowls imported from China and England. Probably made in New England, c. 1790–1810.*

10. *Albert Gallatin, secretary of the Treasury under President Jefferson and financier of the New Geneva, Pennsylvania, glasshouse, graduated from the College of Geneva in 1779. It seems likely this "Achievement" medal was his, as he is known to have won one upon graduation. The goblet, c. 1798, descended in the family of a close friend of Gallatin's.*

Many of the English colonies in North America chafed under the various restrictions placed upon them by the government in London. The increased taxation in the period after 1765 was only one of the irritations that finally led to violence in 1775 and the Declaration of Independence in 1776. The resulting Revolutionary War, which dragged on for seven years, was disastrous for manufacturers whose products were not connected with the war effort. The difficulties faced by Wistar and Stiegel were due in part to the economic upheavals preceding the conflict. The need for glass was so strong that in spite of these difficulties, five glass factories were started during the conflict. None survived the war.

Johann Friedrich Amelung, another German entrepreneur, was the founder of the most important glass factory opened in America in the years immediately following the Revolutionary War. He came to Maryland in 1784 determined to develop a large glass factory complex for the manufacture of all types of glassware. Born in 1741, he was the younger brother of Anton C. F. Amelung, who leased the Duke of Brunswick's mirror factory at Grünenplan, near Hannover, from 1773 until 1789. Anton had no known experience in making glass or managing a glasshouse, and neither did Johann when he joined his brother there in 1773. The younger Amelung was employed for 11 years at Grünenplan, where he apparently learned to manage the glass factory. The Duke of Brunswick's managers demanded unrealistic profits from the enterprise, however. Eventually, Johann left for the New World, and Anton, after a few more years of struggling on his own, gave up the lease. He had previously established contacts in St. Petersburg, and in the early 1780s, he supplied the majority of the mirrors used in Russia. In 1789, he went to Dorpat in Livlund, where he established an extensive mirror factory that operated for many years.

John Frederick Amelung, as he wrote his name in America, found backers among the merchants of Bremen, who supplied him with capital of 10,000 pounds sterling to finance a glass factory and village in the new republic. With this money, he hired workmen, bought equipment for three furnaces, and secured passage to the United States. His choice of Maryland as the site of his factory may seem odd at first, since it was not close to the largest American cities of Boston, Philadelphia, or New York, but he was undoubtedly attracted by Maryland's large tracts of forested land; forests (for fuel) were vital to all successful 18th- and early 19th-century American glass factories.

Amelung arrived in Maryland in August 1784, and within a short time he had purchased a glasshouse started by some of Stiegel's workmen who had migrated to Frederick County, about 40 miles west of Baltimore. The location was excellent, with large supplies of wood and sand, as well as access to the Monocacy and Potomac rivers and a toll road (the National Road) to transport the finished goods to market. Like Pennsylvania, Maryland had a large group of German settlers, and this, too, must have been an attraction. Within a few months, Amelung advertised that window glass and green and white hollow ware were for sale at his "New Bremen Glass-manufactory." He built houses for his workmen near the factory, and a school for their children, just as he and his brother had done at Grünenplan. This was one of the first planned industrial villages in the United States. Amelung eventually purchased thousands of acres of land to ensure his fuel supply.

11. As settlers moved inland, glass factories were established along the major trading routes—rivers, canals, and roads—to meet their needs. Because glassmakers moved frequently, carrying their tools and skills, it is difficult to be certain where many pieces were made. This footed bowl, attributed to New Geneva Glass Works, c. 1798–1819, was made from the type of glass used for windows or bottles.

12. Serving pieces for the table, such as sugar bowls and cream jugs, were often made in American bottle and window glasshouses. Drinking glasses such as this goblet, probably Marlboro Street Glass Works, Keene, N.H., c. 1820–1840, are rare. The dark green and amber glass available to the glassblowers was presumably considered unsuitable.

13. The glass used to make this bowl and pitcher set is the kind that was used for windows. The maker employed applied decorations resembling lily pads. Lily-pad decoration was produced at several American factories. It has no direct European precedents, and is considered an American design innovation. This set may have been made by a glassmaker as a present for a member of his family or a close friend. Until recently, American and European glassmakers were allowed to make objects on their own time using factory glass at no cost. These "end-of-day" objects are among the most fanciful creations made in American glasshouses. This set, made at the Saratoga Glass Works, Mount Pleasant, N.Y., c. 1844–1865, may have been intended for washing the hands in the bedchamber, but apparently it was more admired than used (judging by the lack of wear inside the bowl), which may have contributed to its survival.

14. This vase was undoubtedly made at a window-glass factory. The aqua color would have not been apparent in thinly blown window sheets. Because glassworkers moved frequently, it is often impossible to attribute tableware, such as this, to specific glasshouses. Probably New York, possibly southern New Jersey, c. 1835–1860.

Probably to attract public attention, Amelung made a series of elaborately engraved glasses for various influential politicians and merchants between 1788 and 1792. Many of these glasses were dated and fully signed with the factory name; in several cases, the location of the factory was also given. At least one and perhaps two or more engraved goblets (figure 6) were sent to Amelung's financial backers in Bremen. In addition to these wares, Amelung made ordinary table glass, including decanters, wineglasses, and tumblers (figure 7), which he sold through agents in New York, Philadelphia, Baltimore, and Frederick-Town.

Unfortunately, Amelung seems to have expanded too fast. He built four factories, and in 1790 he claimed to employ between 400 and 500 people. In mid-April of that year, high winds collapsed four houses on the property and may have damaged one of the glasshouses; three weeks later, a warehouse and one of the factories burned down. These difficulties, combined with competition from cheap imported glass and a lack of support from the new

United States government, eventually drove Amelung into bankruptcy. By 1795, the New Bremen Glassmanufactory was closed. This view of the situation, written by a Pennsylvanian in 1795, probably best explains why Amelung failed: "Most new works, have been begun too large in this country. . . . If we built a glass house, it was at the expense of thousands, and calculated to cover all that part of the country with glass which was not covered by houses."

The Revolutionary War, which ended in 1783, had removed official restraints on manufacturing, thus encouraging the development and growth of new industries. However, manufacturers still had to compete with goods from abroad, and the British were especially eager to preserve their markets and to discourage American manufacturing. Except for Amelung's ambitious venture and a short-lived factory in Philadelphia, the managers of glasshouses started in the 1780s and 1790s were content to manufacture windows and bottles, leaving the tableware market to importers. In southern New Jersey, the Stanger family, who had worked for Richard Wistar, started a bottle glasshouse in Glassboro in 1781. Although it changed hands several times, the factory remained in operation for decades. Two glasshouses were started in upstate New York near newly settled areas, and the Pitkin brothers opened a bottle manufactory in 1787 in East Hartford, Connecticut. A particular type of ribbed flask (figure 8) has since acquired their name. This type, blown with a double gather of glass for strength (a German technique), was undoubtedly made in several glasshouses along the East Coast.

The Boston Crown Glass Company was organized in 1788 by several merchants; they were prodded by

15. The hollow knop in the stem of this vase contains a U.S. silver half dime dated 1849. Probably southern New Jersey, c. 1849–1860.

Robert Hewes, who had started an unsuccessful glasshouse in Temple, New Hampshire, several years earlier. The Boston venture did not actually produce glass (figure 9) until 1793, but it remained in business well into the next century and shipped its "Boston Crown" window glass all over the Eastern Seaboard. The difficulty of finding glassblowers is evidenced by the fact that the stockholders advanced Hewes money for a trip to the south to hire workmen. Whether he was successful in luring any away from Amelung or the Stanger factory is not known.

After the Revolutionary War, American settlers moved west in a steady stream, lured by the promise of free land available to those enterprising enough to clear it. It is not surprising that glassworkers were among the pioneers heading west. The price of the commonest household goods was greatly increased by the fact that freight charges were 5 to 10 dollars per 100 pounds for shipments carried over the mountains in wagons or by trains of packhorses. This provided an irresistible impetus for manufacturers of pottery, metals, and glassware in the western settlements, who could compete favorably with goods shipped in from eastern cities. Window glass was especially prone to breakage during shipment, and it was thus one of the products made in the first glasshouse west of the Alleghenies, in western Pennsylvania. That factory, opened in 1797, was financed by Albert Gallatin.

Gallatin was from Geneva, Switzerland. He came to Pennsylvania in 1780, and by 1797 he owned large tracts of property in the western part of the state and was a member of the United States House of Representatives. A financial genius, he served as secretary of the Treasury from 1801 to 1814, reducing the national debt and lowering taxes; he later served as minister to France and to Great Britain. The glassblowers he and his partners employed were experienced Germans who had previously worked for Amelung. In 1804, the glasshouse was moved across the river to Greensboro, where it utilized abundant local coal for fuel and produced window glass until 1847. Tableware was made in both factories using the green glass meant for windows and bottles (figures 10 and 11).

In 1797, another western entrepreneur, the Pittsburgh businessman General James O'Hara, started a

16. Large drinking vessels were necessary items in early 19th-century America as beer and corn whiskey were consumed in enormous quantities. This tankard, c. 1860–1870, is decorated with a dragged white wave pattern. Such decoration is found on English and German glass, as well as on American glass usually attributed to New Jersey and to Pittsburgh, Pennsylvania.

14

bottle manufactory in that city in partnership with Isaac Craig. O'Hara later said facetiously that the first bottle cost the owners $10,000 to produce, indicating the immense sums required to start a glasshouse on the frontier. The factory was ultimately successful, however, and like Gallatin's glasshouse, it operated well into the 19th century.

Throughout the first half of the 19th century, window and bottle glasshouses continued to be concentrated in the heavily forested areas of New England, upstate New York, and southern New Jersey. They were usually located near transportation routes such as rivers and canals, and only occasionally were they found in or near the larger cities. Few were successful, however, as the technology to melt glass and the initial investment required were considerable. Many of the blowers employed in these factories were of German origin. There were no glass factories in the southeastern United States, which had an agrarian economy.

In many of these glasshouses, the blowers made tableware from time to time, either for sale or for the use of their own families. These objects were produced from the dark amber or green bottle glass (figure 12) or from the light aquamarine glass used for making windows, and they were usually the sort of useful forms found around a country home: milk pans, cream jugs and sugar bowls, bowls and pitchers of various sizes (figure 13), and occasionally decorative vases (figures 13, 14 and 15). Although the windows and bottles, which were the formal output of each factory, were usually shipped to cities for sale, the tableware was mostly used locally.

Because these pieces were not made as commercial products, their symmetry and style varied according to the skill and experience of the maker.

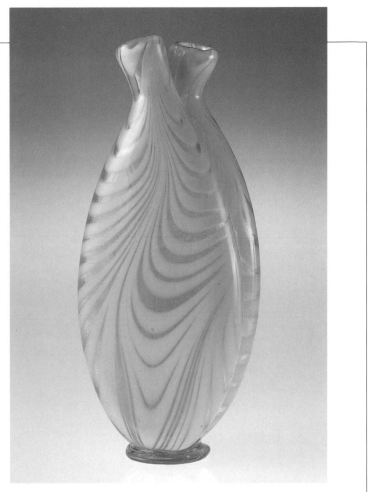

17. These double bottles were usually for oil and vinegar. "Gemel" means coupled, or paired. The name is thought to derive from the Gemini, the heavenly twins in the Zodiac. Eastern United States, c. 1830–1860.

Many of them, however, are among the most attractive American glass objects produced in the second quarter of the 19th century. They often featured applied decoration in the form of lily pads (figure 13), threading, bird finials, and loopings of glass in contrasting colors (figures 15–17). Attributions to particular glasshouses are often impossible, since the glass was never signed and many of the blowers moved from factory to factory in search of better wages and working conditions.

3

Independence Achieved

18. *Sulphides are ceramic compositions inspired by cameos. When molded and fired, they may be encased in glass. They frequently have a silvery appearance because of a layer of air trapped around the sulphide. They were produced in great quantities in England, France, Bohemia, and Russia during the early 19th century. In America, portraits of John Adams and George Washington, De Witt Clinton (governor of New York), Lafayette, and Benjamin Franklin were produced in Pittsburgh. They were mentioned in newspaper advertisements there in 1824, and in 1828 examples were presented with pride to Jackson and Clinton. This tumbler, with a sulphide portrait of President Andrew Jackson in the base, was made by Bakewell, Page & Bakewell, Pittsburgh, Pennsylvania, c. 1824.*

Although Britain signed trade agreements with its former colonies in 1790, American manufacturers were not freed from ruinous foreign competition until the Acts of Embargo and the War of 1812 between England and the United States cut off the supply of British goods. At least 63 glass factories were started between 1790 and 1820. One European traveler wrote: "It is only necessary to reflect upon the situation of the United States. They have immense forests to clear, consequently it is highly proper that they should establish glass manufactories, and increase them as much as possible. The labour employed to destroy the wood for the clearing of lands, at the same time that it disposes

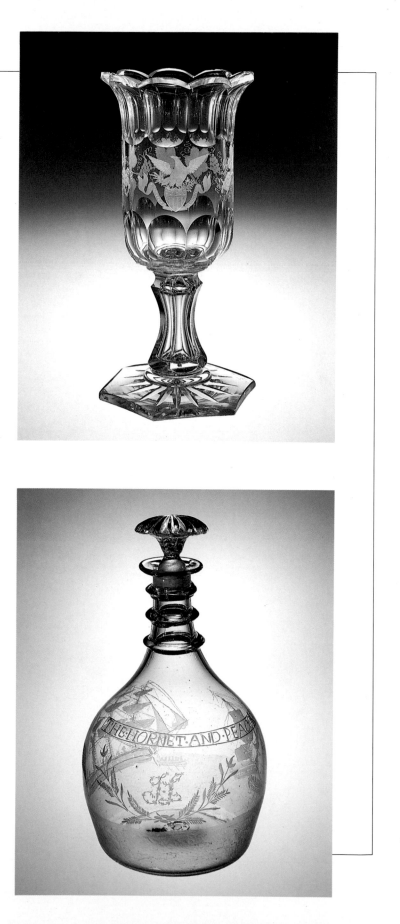

19. The first glass service for official use in the President's House (the White House) was ordered by President James Monroe in 1818 from Bakewell, Page & Bakewell. So much of this was broken during President Andrew Jackson's 1829 inaugural reception that he ordered a second state service from the same maker. This celery vase is presumed to be from that second service. Celery was an exotic vegetable in the early 19th century, often grown in hothouses, and the whole bunch was displayed upright with leaves in a vase like this. If a centerpiece was needed, the celery vase and its contents often served that purpose.

the land to [agri]culture, will serve for the production of a very extensive object of manufacture, therefore the utility of this destruction is double to the Americans. It cannot be doubted, that this consideration will strike them, that they will one day conceive the project of furnishing Europe with glass-ware."

Like most beginning industries, glassmaking was subject to outside influences beyond the control of the manufacturers. For years, craftsmen and factory owners had been unsuccessful in petitioning Congress to impose protective tariffs. The Napoleonic Wars and British interference with American shipping before and during the War of 1812 finally accomplished (at least for a short period) what Congress had failed to do: protect local industries from foreign competition. The near stoppage of imported goods brought many merchants to the brink of

20. The engraved decoration depicts a famous naval engagement during the War of 1812 between the United States and Great Britain. The victorious American Hornet is shown standing alongside the sinking Peacock, a British warship. The decanter, inscribed "J. L.," was made for John Leaugeay, the son-in-law of one of the factory's owners, Charles Ihmsen, at the Birmingham Glass Works, Pittsburgh, Pennsylvania, c. 1813.

17

bankruptcy, as it left them nothing to sell. However, if their capital was not being used to restock their shelves, it was available to invest in manufactures at home, which could then supply the retailers with new stocks for sale.

Imported goods were again available in 1815, and more than half of the operating glassworks failed by 1820, partly due to the export bounty the British government paid glass manufacturers (enabling them to undersell American factories) and to the eagerness of the buying public for the consumer goods in short supply during the War of 1812. It was not until 1824 that a protective tariff was enacted. However, the doubling of the American population between 1800 and 1820 ensured a steady demand for manufactured goods and, eventually, a healthy economy.

In 1809, Congress requested a survey of manufactures. When the results were tabulated several years later, the section on glassmaking indicated that only about half of the window glass then needed could be supplied domestically and that the chief obstacle to the expansion of the glass industry was the scarcity of experienced workmen. Even when glass and other

22. This compote, probably from Pittsburgh, Pennsylvania, was made of transparent amethyst lead glass, about 1840–1860.

goods could be produced in the United States, the lack of easy transportation limited the market sharply. During the period from 1800 to 1830, there was a great increase in the number of toll roads and canals, which, with the advent of the steamboat, helped to alleviate this situation. In 1825, the opening of the Erie Canal made navigation possible from the Atlantic to the Great Lakes, and speeded waves of immigrants on their way inland from the old settlements of New England and the East Coast.

Perhaps this explains why the first manufactory of lead-glass tableware in the new republic was located in Pittsburgh rather than in one of the older East Coast cities. The distance from foreign competition, as well as the availability of customers and of coal for

24. This pitcher, probably from Pittsburgh, Pennsylvania, was made of transparent light violet lead glass, about 1840–1860.

23. As settlers moved west toward the Mississippi River, glass-houses were erected along the migration routes. Raw materials and fuel were found in abundance. The products, such as this covered sugar bowl and cream jug, are frequently strongly colored—amber, green, purple, blue—suitable to a rougher style of living. There were several factories in Ohio. White Glass Works, Zanesville, Ohio, c. 1815–1830.

25. The heavy, broad panels of this pitcher are characteristic of American cut glass made in the East and Midwest. The Sweeney factory made a famous punch bowl, 5 feet high, cut in the same broad panels. Possibly Sweeney's Glass Works, Wheeling, West Virginia, c. 1830–1850.

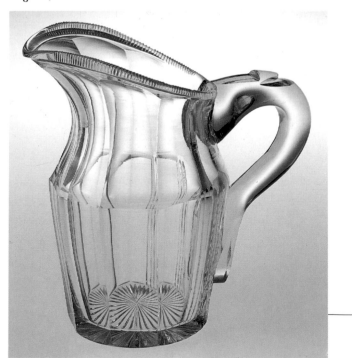

26. *Flasks made in Ohio were often very large, sometimes holding as much as a quart. Whether they were meant as pocket bottles is unknown, although their flattened shapes suggest that they may have been used that way. Corn whiskey was the most popular and prevalent alcoholic beverage there. White Glass Works, Zanesville, Ohio, c. 1815–1830.*

27. *This bottle was made of transparent cornflower blue glass, probably in Zanesville, Ohio, about 1835–1850.*

fuel, may have prompted Benjamin Bakewell, a Pittsburgh merchant, to start a tableware factory in 1808. He advertised his wares widely and was successful financially (figures 18 and 19). Bakewell, who advocated protective tariffs, presented elegant cut decanters to Presidents James Madison and James Monroe when they visited Pittsburgh in 1816 and 1817. Both were strong supporters of American industry. When Monroe ordered furnishings for the President's House in Washington, he included a set of English-style cut glassware from Bakewell's factory. A traveler to Pittsburgh in 1817 wrote that he had seen a pair of decanters, cut in a London pattern, which were indistinguishable from the British original.

Bakewell's was not the only tableware glasshouse

in Pittsburgh; within a few years, there were six others producing good-quality glassware (figure 20). Among the tableware particularly associated with the Pittsburgh area are those pieces with pillar molding, heavy, vertical ribbing that both strengthened and decorated the objects (figures 21, 22, 24). These are thought to have been created for use on the lavish Ohio River steamboats, where sturdy serving pieces were essential. They were probably used in inns and taverns on shore as well.

Down the Ohio River in western Virginia, there were several glasshouses in Wellsburg and Wheeling that also made blown and cut tableware (figure 25). In Ohio, small glass factories operated in Zanesville, Kent, Mantua, and Cincinnati for several years, mak-

29. *This sugar bowl, c. 1813–1829, descended in the family of the manager of the South Boston Flint Glass Works, Thomas Cains. He may have made it to mark his first year with the factory. The form of this piece and its horizontal ribbing are closely allied to contemporary objects produced in England.*

28. *The ovoid, spirally ribbed container has a narrow opening in the top. A coin inside this bank, c. 1840–1845, would have been difficult to retrieve, for the decorative straps across the top restrict access by knives and other slender tools. The ribbing may have encouraged youngsters to save coins by giving the impression that more money was being saved than was actually inside the bank. The only coin in the piece today is a U.S. silver half dime dated 1840, which is imprisoned in the hollow knop of the stem.*

30. *This covered sugar bowl was made by the New England Glass Company, East Cambridge, Massachusetts. A closely related sugar bowl and creamer (at Corning) descended in the family of Thomas Leighton, who was an early superintendent of the New England Glass Company. They were made for a wedding in 1838. Another related creamer in the Henry Ford Museum in Dearborn, Michigan, has a coin dated 1831 in its stem.*

31. The name "Thomas Leighton," cut into the marble base, is that of the superintendent of the New England Glass Company from 1826 until his death in 1849. The solar lamp was probably a gift in appreciation of his service to the company, perhaps in 1846 on the 20th anniversary of his employment. It is one of the earliest known American examples of overlay glass. The "solar" burner was patented in 1843 and, as it gave a brighter light than ordinary whale oil lamps, was very popular until it was superseded by the introduction of kerosene in the 1860s.

32. Whaling was a mainstay of the New England economy during the first half of the 19th century. Oil obtained from the sperm whale was used in lamps, even though the amount of light was only about the same as a candle and the burning fuel gave off an unpleasant smell. Nevertheless, this oil was the most popular lighting fuel in America until the 1860s. The simple metal burner with two wicks would have given about as much light as three candles. The upturned foot rim was probably designed to catch drips in order to protect furniture and fabrics.

ing a variety of tableware and bottles (figures 23, 26–28). The Ohio glasshouses were adjacent to the new lands being opened for settlement, and since tableware of any material was scarce, the manufacturers found a ready market. One traveler described it graphically: "The furniture for the table is equally scanty and inconvenient. . . . Articles of crockery are few and indifferent. . . . For want of a glass . . . from which to drink, if you are offered whisky (which is the principal drink here) the bottle is presented to you or a bowl or a teacup containing the liquor."

Dwellers in the Eastern Seaboard cities had easier access to imported wares, but locally made tableware was also available. Thomas Cains, who worked for the Boston Crown Glass Manufactory, began blowing lead glass tableware (figure 29) during the War of 1812. He eventually formed his own firm, the Phoenix Glass Works, which was in business until 1870. In 1818, a group of investors opened the New England Glass Company, an East Cambridge, Massa-

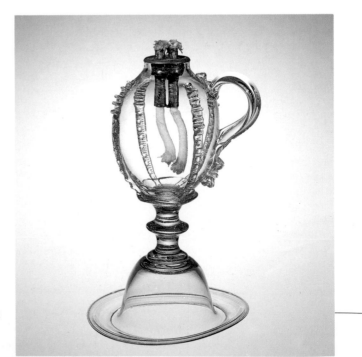

chusetts, factory that was destined to operate for most of the 19th century. Within a few years the company employed about 140 men, and it eventually became one of the largest and most successful glass factories in the United States. In a period when most manufacturing concerns probably employed fewer than 20 people, this was a business giant. The New England Glass Company made all types of tableware and lighting devices (figures 30 and 31). In 1825 Deming Jarves, who had been an agent for the New England Glass Company, started the Boston & Sandwich Glass Company in Sandwich, Massachusetts. This factory, too, survived for most of the 19th century. These three Boston-area glasshouses made the same sorts of tableware, using the same techniques and in some cases sharing workmen and selling agents. Thus, it is often impossible to distinguish the products of one factory from those of another (figures 32–34).

By 1830, the New York City area had become the mercantile capital of the new country. It had several glasshouses producing fine tableware; two of these factories had been started by workmen from the New England Glass Company. In 1824, Phineas and George Dummer, who had been china and glassware sellers in New York City, started their own glass factory (figure 35) in Jersey City, New Jersey, in association with an earthenware factory.

In Philadelphia, several bottle glasshouses were in

33. The origin of this vase and of others like it is uncertain. They are of high-quality, brilliantly colored lead glass, and the panel molding has English precedents. However, the form is not found in English glass so we assume it to be American. Probably Boston area, c. 1825–1850.

34. Originally, most cut glass whale oil or fluid lamps probably had shades, as this one does. The shades were easily broken, however, and have rarely survived. They served both to protect the flame from drafts and to diffuse the light which was considered too strong by those used to candles. New England, c. 1830–1840.

23

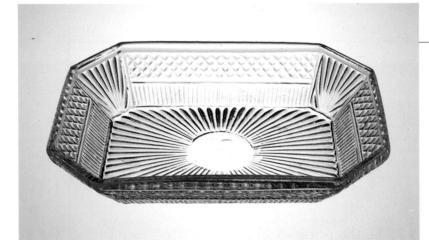

38. *Blown in a mold which gave it a decorative pattern and shape, this bowl is an example of an early attempt at mass production. Such molded pieces were much less expensive than the blown and cut pieces they imitated. However, except for tumblers and bottles, most forms still required considerable hand-shaping. Probably New England Glass Company, Cambridge, or Boston and Sandwich Glass Company, Sandwich, Massachusetts, c. 1818–1830.*

population had increased to 23 million and the nation extended all the way to the Pacific Ocean. The northeastern United States was still the most heavily populated area and the center of most industry; the South and the West were largely agricultural. In the expanding economy, employment opportunities were readily available and an increasing proportion of the population was able to afford more than the bare necessities of life.

The growing population of the United States meant more buyers for glassware, and the rise both in the number of middle-class families and in the buying power of the average family added greatly to the market for manufactured goods. These factors created a much higher demand for glass of all types. Because the manufacture and decoration of hand-blown tableware were slow and costly, early 19th-century European and American manufacturers sought ways to speed production and to decorate

their glass more cheaply. One way to do this was to blow the gather of glass into a full-sized mold, producing the shape and surface decoration in one operation. Time and money were saved because the object did not need to be formed by hand or decorated by cutting or engraving. This technique was introduced in the manufacture of European and American tableware early in the 19th century (figures 37–41). A book published in New York in 1815 suggested that housewives seeking elegant and fashionable dishes that cost less than cut glass objects should buy molded wares.

In addition, the molds could be used to make more than one object: pitchers were usually shaped in decanter molds, tumblers were turned into mugs by the addition of handles, and stopper molds were used to make the fonts of tiny bedside lamps. The first patterns used were copies of cut glass then in vogue, and they were mostly geometric. Once the

39. *This colorless lead glass punch bowl was probably made at the Boston and Sandwich Glass Company, Sandwich, Massachusetts, c. 1825–1840.*

40. *The Boston and Sandwich Glass Company in Sandwich, Massachusetts, is known to have made quantities of this molded ware. Other companies also made it but no evidence exists to attribute most of the patterns to specific companies, c. 1825–1840.*

mold-blown glassware had become popular, manufacturers made use of other decorative elements, including curves and scrolls. Most of this glassware was colorless, like the cut glass it often imitated. However, a few pitchers and decanters are found in rich blue, amber, or amethyst glass (figure 41). All of the eastern tableware factories advertised "moulded glassware," but for some inexplicable reason the table glass factories in Pittsburgh and West Virginia seem never to have adopted this technique, which was popular from about 1812 until about 1840.

A related technique was used to produce pocket flasks for whiskey and other spirits during the same period. Patterned and plain ovoid flasks (or pocket bottles as they were often called in advertisements) had been made in Europe since at least the 17th century. Around 1815, glass manufacturers in America began to form flasks in full-sized molds that gave a pattern to the sides as well as standard capacities. One of the problems with flasks had been their lack of accurate volume measurements; with the full-sized molds, sellers could advertise that their containers held exact pints or quarts, thereby increasing the sale of spirits by the bottle (rather than by the barrel or cask). Corn, the grain from which whiskey was made, was an important cash crop, and on the frontier, the easiest way to get the grain to market was as a concentrate, distilled and barreled. Thus, both farmers and glassmakers were dependent upon whiskey for a portion of their profits. In some inland

41. *This colorless lead glass pitcher was made about 1825–1840 at the Boston and Sandwich Glass Company, Sandwich, Massachusetts.*

42. This flask commemorates the 50th anniversary of the Declaration of Independence and the nearly simultaneous deaths of Presidents John Adams and Thomas Jefferson on July 4, 1826. The flask also bears the initials of the owner of the Kensington Glass Works, Dr. Thomas W. Dyott. Whiskey was the most common drink in the United States in the early 19th century, and more than 600 different designs for whiskey flasks were made. Because of their decoration, many were cherished possessions in an era when most table glass was expensive and hard to obtain.

43. The figure of Columbia wearing a liberty cap was popular as an emblem for the United States in the late 18th century. The national symbol, in widespread use after its adoption for the Great Seal of the United States, can be seen on the reverse of the flask: the heraldic American eagle holding a thunderbolt, arrows, and an olive branch—symbols of war and peace—in its talons. Union Glass Works, Kensington, Philadelphia, c. 1826–1830.

areas where currency was scarce, whiskey was used in place of money.

Within a few years, these decorative flasks became extremely popular with manufacturers and consumers alike. More than 600 different designs, produced between about 1815 and 1865, have been identified. Most of them were made of greenish or amber nonlead glass. Almost every bottle glasshouse produced one or more patterned mold-blown flasks. Decorative motifs included portraits of political candidates and military heroes such as George Washington (figure 42) and Zachary Taylor, nationalistic symbols of the United States such as Columbia (figure 43) and the American eagle (figures 42, 43, 46), sunbursts and scrolls, various forms of transportation (figure 45), national monuments, and foreign visitors (figure 44). Masonic symbols (figure 46), found on many flasks, are a reminder that Freemasonry (a fraternal, protective, and benevolent so-

44. *The Hungarian freedom fighter Louis Kossuth, who is portrayed on this bottle, visited the United States in 1851–52 to gather support for Hungarian independence from Austria. His cause gained popular support but the U.S. government remained strictly neutral. The ship on which his party arrived, the steam frigate U.S.S.* Mississippi, *is shown on the reverse. The bottle was presumably made for a Philadelphia glass merchant, Samuel Huffsey, whose name is inscribed below the ship. Although there were many independent mold makers like Doflein, few marked their molds for purposes of advertisement, as was done in this case. Probably Millford Glass Works, Millford, N.J., c. 1851–1855.*

45. *This flask depicts a horse-drawn cart that runs on iron rails. Another version of the flask shows a steam-powered locomotive, which was first used in the United States in 1831. Marlboro Street Glass Works, Keene, New Hampshire, c. 1830–1840.*

ciety) was a powerful influence on American life throughout the 19th century.

Although patterning and shaping blown glass in molds was an efficient method of mass production, a number of American glassmakers experimented with other methods to reduce costs and speed production even more. One result was the pressing or casting of glass in molds. This was not an altogether new technique in the 1820s; its ancestry can be traced back to ancient times, when pendants and inlays were cast in open molds as early as the 16th century B.C. The principle of squeezing rather than blowing glass into a shape had also been practiced in Europe since the early 18th century, when salts and chandelier prisms were made that way. By the latter part of the century, decanter stoppers and bases for lamps, goblets, compotes, salts, and other small articles were being made by this process in England. These bases usually were very simple, often square,

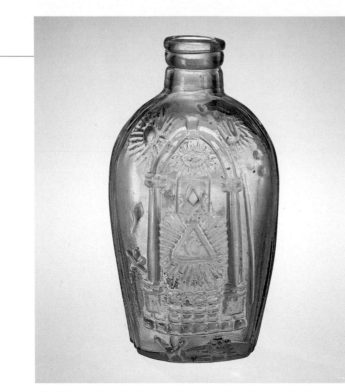

46. *The molded details on this masonic and eagle flask are secret symbols of the fraternity of Freemasons. The organization began in the late Middle Ages as an association of stonemasons—thus the name. By the 17th century it was purely a social organization, and was brought to the American colonies early in the 18th century. By 1734, it is estimated, there were some 6,000 Masons here, and in the mid-20th century there were about 4 million. Every U.S. president from George Washington to Harry Truman was a Mason. New England, c. 1818–1825.*

inventor remains a mystery. The process was probably developed gradually by several people, each of whom added improvements. By 1829, it was so well advanced that when James Boardman, an English traveler, visited an exhibition of American manufactured goods, he commented: "The most novel article was the pressed glass, which was far superior, both in design and execution, to anything of the kind I have ever seen in London or elsewhere. The merit of its invention is due to the Americans and it is likely to prove one of great national importance."

Boardman was an accurate prophet. Within a few years many companies were using the new technique, and large quantities of pressed glass tableware were being exported to Europe, the Caribbean, and South America. By 1840 the patterned mold-blown tableware that had been introduced just a few years earlier was completely outmoded by the newer technology of pressing.

47. *Many early pressed-glass tablewares imitated the more expensive cut glass. New England, c. 1830–1835.*

perhaps with a concave rosette or fluted design on the bottom; like the ancient objects, many were finished by wheel-polishing the edges. These pieces were relatively common in England, and some were made in the United States. However, since the bowls of the goblets, compotes, lamps, and salts were blown and were often decorated with cutting or engraving, they were not necessarily inexpensive.

The process of pressing molten glass in metal molds by machine was perfected first in the United States between 1820 and 1825, but the identity of the

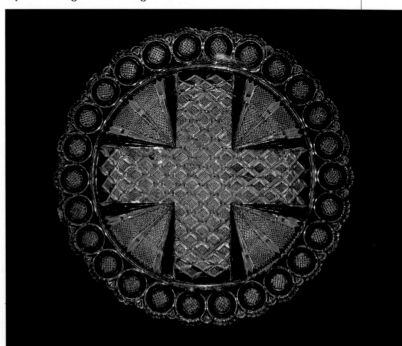

Nevertheless, there were difficulties in perfecting the new process. In order to keep the glass from sticking to the metal molds and to get a clear impression of the pattern, the molds had to be preheated and then kept at a uniformly high temperature. If the temperature of the mold fell much below that of the molten glass, the outermost layer of the glass would chill too quickly and the surface would be dull and wrinkled. Contact with the mold destroyed the surface gloss of the finished piece in any case. To mask this problem, the molds were patterned in intricate stippled, "lacy" designs that formed tiny raised bumps on the outside of the glass. Thus, light passing through the glass and reflecting off the stipples distracted the eye from the wrinkled surface.

It was also necessary for the workman to cut off exactly the right amount of molten glass to fill all the recesses of the mold. If he cut off too little, handles and knobs would be incomplete; if he cut off too much, the piece would have fins on the rim, or it would be too thick.

Some of the earliest pressed patterns were derived from cut glass, still the most fashionable type of glass (figures 47 and 48). Other designs were copied from architectural pattern books and utilized Gothic arches (figure 49), acanthus leaves, scrolls (figures 50 and 51), and other elements fashionable in interior decoration. Stylized floral designs may have been copied from English transfer-printed ceramics that were being exported to the United States in tremendous quantities.

Making a metal mold was a complex process. First, a wooden model of the desired object was made. Next, a plaster model of the metal mold, with interlocking lugs and hinges, was formed around the wooden model. A sand mold was then made around

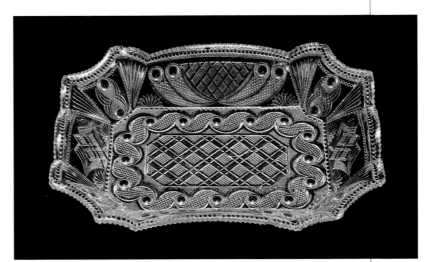

48. The mechanical pressing of molten glass into molds was developed in the United States in the 1820s. It was probably the most important American contribution to glassmaking since it led eventually to high-speed mass production in the early 20th century. Mass production of pressed tableware meant that glass serving pieces were suddenly available to the average American family instead of being affordable only to the prosperous. The earliest designs were often stippled with intricate "lacy" designs that disguised the wrinkled surface. New England, c. 1830–1840.

49. Colored "lacy" pressed glass is extremely rare. More than a dozen examples of this casket are known in colorless lead glass, but this is the only colored one known. New England, c. 1835–1840.

50. *This compote was made in New England, c. 1830–1845, in colorless, yellow, amethyst, and blue glass. Most early pressed designs were available only in colorless glass. This is another design that was copied by the Meissen porcelain factory.*

51. *Several early pressed patterns were copied from British earthenware shapes. In the early 1830s the Meissen porcelain factory in Germany copied the American design of this tray in hard-paste porcelain. New England, c. 1830–1840.*

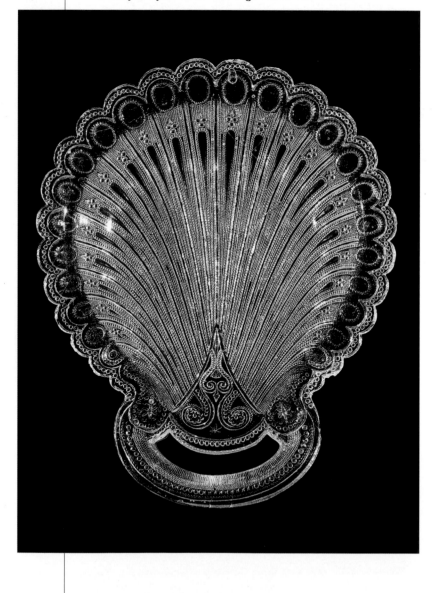

the plaster model, and an iron or brass mold was cast from it. The fine details of the pattern were hand-finished by a diesinker. Today, the identity of individual mold makers is uncertain, and it seems unlikely that any of the glass companies employed specialist designers. Smaller companies must have ordered the expensive metal molds from independent mold shops, but the larger firms, such as the New England Glass Company and Bakewell, Page & Bakewell, probably had mold makers on the premises.

Identifying the manufacturers of many of the earliest pressed patterns is also difficult because so few pieces were signed. In addition, many firms copied one another's popular patterns. Copying was a widespread practice in New England in the late 1820s. It is likely that glassmakers in Pittsburgh were doing the same thing, thereby making absolute identification of most early pressed glass nearly impossible today.

The development of the mechanical press led not only to faster production but also to a variety of new

52. *Cup plates were used in the United States from about 1825 until 1865 to hold a teacup while the tea was poured into the saucer to cool. The tea was then sipped from the saucer. This fashion seems to have been popular only in the United States. Several hundred different patterns of cup plates were made at many different factories. Fort Pitt Glass Works, Pittsburgh, Pennsylvania, c. 1830–1845.*

forms. Molds for utilitarian plates and bowls were easily created, and designs proliferated in the 1830s and 1840s. Sugar bowls and cream jugs were also popular products in pressed glass. When first made, their shapes were copied from English earthenware objects, the most popular and affordable tableware among the American middle class. A few of the earliest pieces matched in pattern, but the concept of sets of matching glass tableware, already common in more expensive glass, had not yet reached the pressed-glass market.

Americans drank great quantities of tea in the 19th century, since it was served both with and between meals. Following Oriental prototypes, earthenware and porcelain cups were often made without handles, and the hot tea was commonly poured into deep saucers, from which it was drunk, after cooling. The ungainly fashion was mainly American, and it led to the development of a new form in glass, the cup plate (figure 52). This object was developed to hold the drinker's teacup while the tea was cooling and being sipped from the saucer. Cup plates, which protected the table or tablecloth from dripping tea, were in common use in the United States from about 1829 to 1865, but apparently they were not used in any other country. Most were made of pressed glass, and they were often decorated with political heroes or national emblems

53. *Bar bottles like this were used for serving liquor in a tavern or restaurant and had cork or similar stoppers. They are never ground on the inside of the neck for glass stoppers, as decanters are, because they were used only for serving, not storage. They are usually quite heavy in order to withstand hard use in a commercial establishment. Probably Pittsburgh, Pennsylvania, c. 1855–1870.*

54. Vividly colored glass lamps, candlesticks, and vases were popular household accessories in the mid-19th century. For technical reasons, it was easier to press such a piece in two halves and join them while hot with a wafer of molten glass. New England or Midwest, c. 1840–1860.

similar to those used on whiskey flasks. Like the flasks, cup plates came in a wide variety of colors and patterns. Judging by the enormous number of patterns and the quantity of these plates surviving today, they must have been staple items for every glasshouse making pressed glass.

American glassmakers did not begin to produce matched sets of tableware before the middle of the 19th century. Indeed, pressed drinking glasses were not made prior to about 1837 because of the difficulty in controlling the thickness of the rim and in finishing it smoothly. The requisite for a smooth rim finish was fire-polishing, which involved sticking the glass on a pontil and exposing it to the heat of the furnace just long enough to melt the edge so that it would regain the polish lost by contact with the mold. This was an extra step, which added to the production cost. However, the improving technology that made new and complicated shapes possible around the mid-1800s was accompanied by a shift in taste to simpler, paneled, and fluted decorative patterns (figures 53–55) related to a new fashion in cut glass. Fire-polishing also eliminated the need for the elaborate stippled patterns, and it made the simpler patterns look more like cut glass. The new technology and the new styles developed together, one lending the other a sense of high fashion.

By 1849, pressed-glass table sets were being made. These sets, made in matching patterns, included goblets, wineglasses, egg cups, tumblers, plates, sugar bowls, creamers, celery glasses, spoon holders, water pitchers, decanters, butter dishes, and compotes of several sizes. Every shape of the more expensive cut glass that graced the tables and sideboards of the wealthy was suddenly available to

55. This pattern, named "Argus" by the manufacturer, was made up of repeated oval facets or "eyes" (which prompted the pattern name) that act like small reducing lenses. This punch bowl, made by Bakewell, Pears & Company, Pittsburgh, Pennsylvania, c. 1850–1870, is one of the largest pieces made in America by pressing.

people of lesser means. The popularity of sets was a tremendous boost for glass factories, as it encouraged housewives to buy more and more.

By the middle of the 19th century, the pressing process had become so efficient that a team of five men could make 100 tumblers in an hour. This was several times as fast as blown wares in similar shapes could be turned out. Moreover, because glass pressers did not need the skills of glassblowers, they were paid less; this was another reason factory owners appreciated the new method. The glass industry became less dependent upon finding trained European workmen to come to the United States, and it began to employ unskilled Americans who could be trained quickly as pressers.

Until 1864, glass for pressing was usually lead glass. Lead glass had a number of desirable qualities, among them clarity and brilliance that made objects more attractive. Because it did not harden quickly, it was easy to work. It was expensive to make, however. In 1864, William Leighton of Hobbs, Brockunier &

56. This pattern evokes the American frontier. The finial is in the form of a crouching Indian. The sides of the cover have raised molded decoration of a log cabin, trees, and buffalo. This butter dish was probably made first for the 1876 Centennial Exhibition in Philadelphia by Gillinder & Sons. A number of different shapes, including stemware, bread tray, compotes, sugar bowl, and cream pitcher were made in this pattern.

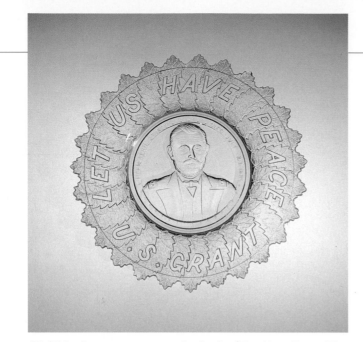

57. *This plate commemorates the death of President Grant. The inscription* "LET US HAVE PEACE" *is a quotation from his speech on May 29, 1868, accepting the nomination for the presidency. He had been commander of the Union armies in the Civil War that ended in 1865. It also bears the dates of his birth and death (1822–1885). Probably Adams & Company, Pittsburgh, Pennsylvania, c. 1885.*

58. *This portrait bust of George Washington was probably made by Bakewell, Pears & Company, Pittsburgh, Pennsylvania, at the time of the centennial of the United States for display and sale at the 1876 Centennial Exhibition in Philadelphia.*

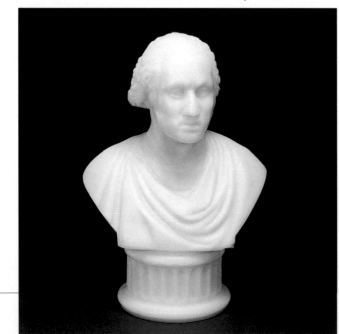

Company in Wheeling, West Virginia, perfected a formula for a soda-lime glass for pressing. This glass was far less expensive to make than lead glass, and thus it improved the competitive position of the factories that produced it. It could be used to make thinner, lighter tableware, which still retained some of the brilliance associated with lead glass. Patterns became flatter and more pictorial (figures 56 and 57). The new formula and the availability of natural gas for fuel gave the western factories an economic edge, and the center of the American glass industry gradually shifted westward from the East Coast. At the international exposition in Philadelphia in 1876, glass manufacturers from western Pennsylvania, West Virginia, and Ohio showed nothing but pressed glass in a variety of naturalistic and often colored patterns (figure 58) that drew admiring comments from the reviewers.

The basic necessities, windowpanes and bottles, were still the mainstay of the glass industry in the late 19th century. For this market, there was much less competition from abroad. However, the growth of manufacturing in the settled Eastern states was drawing Americans in increasing numbers from the farms to towns and cities to work in factories and stores. This did not reverse the traditional migration patterns, which still led to the free land on the western frontier, but it did mean that a larger proportion of the population had increased income, permitting the purchase of larger houses and more elaborate furnishings. The glass industry expanded to supply this market, making pressed tableware, candlesticks (figure 59), and lamps for the middle class and cut glass and more elaborate lighting devices for the increasing number of wealthy citizens.

By the 1870s, candles, which had been the common form of lighting in poorer homes, were almost completely replaced by kerosene lamps that were usually made of glass. Kerosene, refined from petroleum or from coal, became a popular lamp fuel around 1860. It changed the way Americans lighted their homes, and it provided a great market for the glass industry. Whale oil and other fuels had not required lamp chimneys in order to burn (except in the expensive Argand lamps, which were usually imported from England), and chimneys and shades had been used only on elaborate lamps. Kerosene, which was cheap and generally safe to use, required a chimney to burn efficiently. For the glass industry, chimneys were both a new product to sell and a necessity, not a luxury. The production of glass lamps increased tremendously as the new technologies made pressing more and more efficient.

The mid-19th century was a period when railroads began to bring the United States together, when the textile industry developed in New England, and when other traditional crafts began moving from small workshops into factory settings. By 1850 the American glass industry was stable and prosperous, able to fill the demands of an expanding market with quality products. This was due in large measure to the invention of the pressing machine, which brought the benefits of the Industrial Revolution to glassmaking. Mass production was the most important American contribution to the glass industry, and it was a change as far-reaching in its implications as was the invention of the blowpipe centuries earlier.

After the Civil War, mass production made it possible to rely less on trained labor. Unions of glassmakers were organized, and by the 1880s, wages and prices in the glass industry were closely regulated by

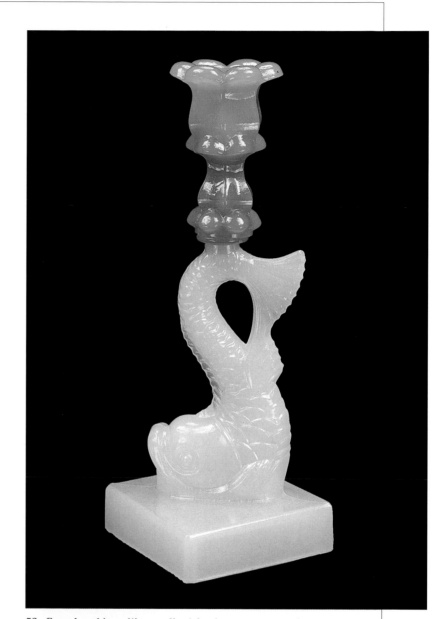

59. *Complex objects like candlesticks, lamps, vases, and compotes had to be pressed in two or three sections, and then the sections were joined with a wafer of molten glass while all the parts were still hot. It took great care to ensure that these pieces were put together straight and not askew. A greater variety of shapes could be made by combining different top and bottom molds. Two-color pieces also added variety to factory production. This dolphin candlestick was made in New England, c. 1840–1860.*

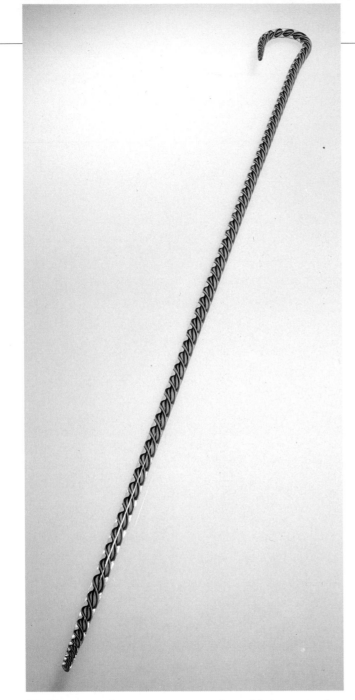

60. *Glass canes, horns, trumpets, swords, and hats were made by glassmakers in Europe and the United States for parades and other festive occasions. This cane, made at the Libbey Glass Company, Toledo, Ohio, is said to have been carried in a Labor Day parade on September 1, 1902, by a member of the American Flint Glass Workers Union in Toledo.*

agreements between the unions and the manufacturers' associations. On Labor Day, a holiday that became official throughout the United States in 1894, members of glassmakers' unions often paraded in the streets with other workers, carrying products of their labor and skill. It was for these annual parades that many glass canes were made (figure 60). Wages were higher than those paid in Europe, so manufacturers were forced to charge higher prices, and there was an increasing use of cheaper child and female labor. Tariffs offered some protection from foreign competition, but imported glass was readily available.

Containers continued to be an important part of the glass industry. In 1880 more than 25 percent of the glass made in the United States was for common bottles, slightly less than that was for windows, and 50 percent was for tableware and better-quality containers. Home preserving of fruits and vegetables—in glass jars made especially for the purpose—became popular in the second half of the century. All sorts of household goods, from food and drink to medicines and hair tonics, were marketed in specially made bottles. Bottles and jars were still produced by blowing into full-size molds and finishing the necks and rims with special tools. Eventually, in the early 1900s, containers were made completely by machine, and even fewer workers were needed than before.

5

Luxury Glass: 1850-1900

61. *This compote descended in the family of Mrs. Charles X. Dalton, who worked as a bookkeeper at the New England Glass Company from 1872 until 1876.*

The Eastern factories switched to coal as wood supplies were depleted in their heavily settled region of the country. Coal had to be transported over considerable distances and was thus much more expensive than the wood had been. Natural gas, which was available in Ohio, Illinois, and other nearby states, was much cheaper than coal (if the coal had to be shipped). Consequently, most of the Eastern companies stopped making pressed glass and concentrated on the market for luxury wares, where the higher manufacturing costs could be passed on more easily to the buyer. From 1855 to 1860, there were about 250 glass cutters working in the United States, most of them in the East.

62. *Louis Vaupel was a copper wheel engraver who emigrated from Germany in 1856 and soon became foreman of the engraving department at the New England Glass Company. He engraved a number of pieces for family members, but this goblet, c. 1870–1875, considered by him to be his masterpiece, he kept for himself. Its hunting scene is characteristic of the pictorial engraved glass popular in Germany. The extremely fine detail in the tiny figures demonstrates Vaupel's mastery of the craft.*

During and after the Civil War (1860–1865), that number declined sharply. Of the more than 40 glass firms that had been founded earlier in the century to produce lead glass, only eight survived in 1865—five in New England and three in the Middle Atlantic states. The economic depression that began in 1873 further reduced the demand for cut glass.

By the middle of the 19th century, strawberry diamond cutting, copied from English glass, had been replaced by paneled, stepped, and fluted cuttings that emphasized the purity of the glass (figure 61). This simpler style was also good for copper-wheel engraving, which increasingly was used to embellish glassware, especially presentation pieces made for special occasions. The cutters were often trained Englishmen who had emigrated to the United States, confident of finding employment at higher salaries than they could get at home. Many of the engravers had been trained in the highly orga-

63. *The building depicted on this goblet is the St. James Hotel in New York City, built as a luxury hotel in 1863. Pieces engraved with buildings like this are also known in English glass and were usually specially ordered, perhaps to commemorate the erection of the building or a notable event. Probably New York City, possibly Christian Dorflinger or John Hoare, c. 1863–1875.*

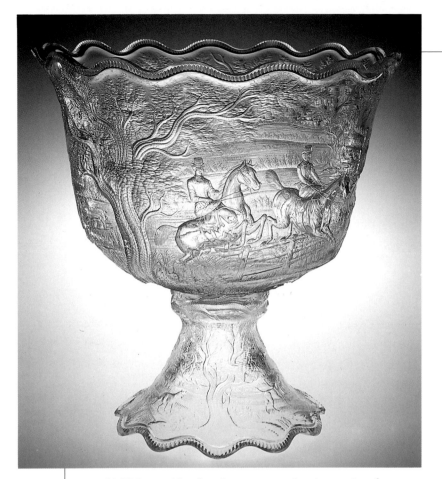

64. *This punchbowl and cups—exceptional examples of engraved glass—were shown in the Libbey Company's exhibit at the Louisiana Purchase Exposition, the world's fair held at St. Louis, Missouri, in 1904.*

65. *This five-piece place setting was part of a 90-piece stemware set made by the Libbey Glass Company, Toledo, Ohio, for the 1904 world's fair in St. Louis. The engraved motifs include stylized orchids alternating with elaborate fleurs-de-lis. The polished "rock crystal" style of engraving found on this set and the punch set (64) is rare in American glass. It was developed in Vienna in the 1870s, copied in England in the 1880s, and finally produced in the United States around 1900. It was never really popular here, perhaps because it was too costly.*

nized German or Bohemian apprentice system. Louis Vaupel, one of the most talented German engravers ever to come to the United States, worked for the New England Glass Company from 1855, when he arrived in the country, until his retirement in 1888. As head of the engraving shop, he used European design motifs in many of his own works (figure 62), and he trained a number of American-born engravers.

Although monograms and inscriptions were popular on glass throughout the 1800s, mid-19th-

century engravers added elaborate floral patterns, views of American scenery and buildings (figure 63), and naturalistic motifs of plants and animals. Engraved glassware remained popular until World War I, but because of the time involved in its production and the high salary of the engravers, it became increasingly expensive. After 1880, polished engraving (figures 64 and 65) was in vogue. This was usually referred to as "rock crystal engraving," likening it to the elaborately carved quartz (rock crystal) pieces made during the 16th and 17th centuries. Previously,

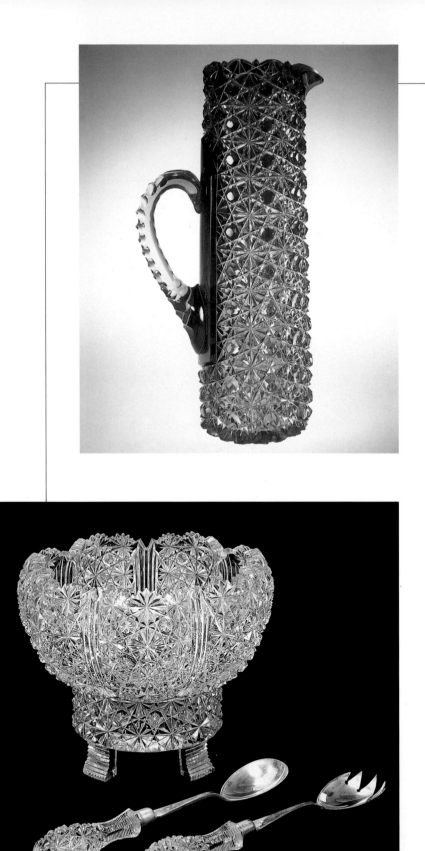

engraving on glass had usually been left matte (with a dull finish).

After the 1840s and 1850s, when heavy pieces cut in simple patterns were popular, tableware became lighter and thinner, and cut patterns became more delicate. Perhaps because this glass was more fragile, the style did not remain popular for long. Heavier glass, deeply cut in intricate patterns on thicker blanks, became popular again in the 1870s. This change was first seen at the 1876 international exposition in Philadelphia, where the exhibits of East Coast glass companies were full of cut and engraved glasses in both the new, heavier style and the older, lightweight one. International expositions were traditionally showcases where manufacturers displayed their best and newest designs, and where consumers came to buy as well as to look. The new fortunes made in railroads, steamships, oil, steel, and other industries created both a new class of millionaires eager to show off their wealth and a large market for luxury goods.

67. A banquet service in this "Russian" pattern is said to have been made by the Hawkes company about 1883–1895 for the Russian Embassy in Washington and another for the American Embassy in St. Petersburg—thus the name of the pattern. Another set of tableware in this style, with an engraved Great Seal of the United States, was made in 1891 for President Benjamin Harrison for use in the White House.

Gillinder & Company of Philadelphia operated a complete glass factory on the 1876 exposition grounds, making and selling popular pressed souvenir pieces as well as cut and engraved glass. The attention that Gillinder's workmen and the displays of cut glass attracted, combined with the growing middle-class prosperity in the United States, led to a boom in the cut glass industry. Orders increased, and cutting shops proliferated all over the United States. The heavy blanks and intricate cuttings and engravings perfectly suited the aspirations of the new American millionaires. Typically, every inch of the surface of an object was decorated—a style that went well with the heavy furniture, patterned fabrics, and rich colors popular at the time (figures 66–71).

One of the earliest of the new style patterns was "Russian," designed in 1882 at the factory of T. G. Hawkes in Corning, New York (figures 66 and 67). The pattern acquired its name in 1885 after the Russian Embassy in Washington and the American Embassy in St. Petersburg acquired sets of the glassware. In 1891, a large "Russian" service decorated with the presidential seal was acquired by President Benjamin Harrison for state dinners at the White House. Although Hawkes had patented the pattern to protect it from competition, the design proved so popular that by 1890 several other glasshouses were

68. *Kerosene banquet lamps in cut glass were among the most expensive shapes made, usually retailing for several hundred dollars. This was about 20 times the weekly wage of the craftsmen who did the cutting. Relatively few were made, and because of their fragility, few have survived. Cut by T. G. Hawkes & Company, Corning, N.Y., c. 1890–1900.*

69. *This vase was cut and engraved about 1911–1920 by Frederick and George Haselbauer as a present for their mother. The Haselbauers had a small cutting and engraving shop and did contract work for larger firms. The combination of geometric and floral decoration was used by only a few American cutting firms.*

70. *This table was made as a spectacular display piece for the Libbey Company exhibit at the Louisiana Purchase Exposition in St. Louis, Missouri, in 1904. Such pieces were often created for display, and if not sold to a wealthy buyer, would remain on view in the company showroom—as did this one.*

producing it, even in Russia. Indeed, many cut glass patterns patented or registered between 1882 and 1915 were quickly copied by rival cutting shops. As this "brilliant" style of cut glass became popular, small cutting shops sprang up all over the United States, and the sheer size of the industry prevented any attempt to stop the pirating of patterns.

Cut glass manufacturers increasingly suffered from foreign competition because European glassblowers and cutters were paid much less than their American counterparts. American cut glass makers also suffered from an oversupply of the product at home and from the competition of cheap pressed copies that were available at a fraction of the cost of cut glass. Gradually, brilliant cut glass lost its pres-

71. Designed by H. P. Sinclaire in 1926, this covered potpourri jar was a special gift for his stepmother. The elaborate engraving was typical of the best work done at the Sinclaire firm. The shape is reminiscent of a Chinese "ginger" jar.

tige, and a new generation of householders looked for something different for their tables.

Glass manufacturers also sought new methods and styles of decoration for their products, as the Victorian idea of "good taste" had become more ornate after the Great Exhibition of 1851 in London. Some glass of this period imitated other substances, such as mercury glass (figure 72), which resembled silver, and "ice glass" (figure 74), which looked like crushed ice. Other glassmakers created new and dramatic color effects. The addition of special ingredients to the mix meant that the finished product could be shaded; reheating portions of the glass caused them to "strike" or change color. This became a popular method of decoration after the New England Glass Company introduced Amberina (figure 66) in 1883. Amberina was an amber glass which, because of the addition of gold to the batch, could be shaded gradually from amber to red if it was reheated carefully during the manufacturing process. It inspired a host of imitators, the most famous of which was Peachblow, an Amberina glass lined with opaque white to give it a porcelainlike appearance. The name was adopted after the sale in 1886 of a Chinese porcelain "peachbloom" vase for the as-

72. Mercury glass was patented by the New England Glass Company in 1855, but the firm had already exhibited "one large silver glass bowl on foot, richly engraved" at the New York Exhibition of 1853. British glassmakers had patented the same process in 1849.

45

73. This "Morgan Vase," made by Hobbs, Brockunier & Company, Wheeling, West Virginia, c. 1886–1891, imitates a famous 18th-century Chinese "peachbloom" porcelain vase from the Mary Morgan collection that was sold at auction in 1886 for the sensationally high price of $18,000. The pressed glass stand imitates the Chinese carved wood stand for the peachbloom vase.

74. There is a reservoir for ice behind the handle of this pitcher, allowing a drink such as champagne to be cooled without dilution by melting ice. Probably Boston and Sandwich Glass Company, Sandwich, or New England Glass Company, East Cambridge, Massachusetts, c. 1870–1888.

tounding price of $18,000. The sale made headlines all over the country, and glass and pottery manufacturers rushed to capitalize on the publicity by making objects in the same shape and with vaguely related colors (figure 73).

The largest manufacturer of art glass was probably the Mount Washington Glass Company of New Bedford, Massachusetts, which marketed quantities of glass with a stained-glass appearance that it called "Royal Flemish" (figure 75), as well as glass enameled to look like porcelain and sold under the trade names of Albertine, Dresden, and Crown Milano (figure 76). This firm also made Burmese, which used uranium and gold to produce a delicate pink-to-yellow color, and some other shaded wares (figures 77 and 78).

Decorative objects made in the glasshouses by workers on their own time used the stripes and loopings of the earlier period, but in late 19th-century colors (figure 79). Paperweights, often enclosing flowers or sentimental messages, were also made by workmen on their own time. Many of these contained lampworked elements that the workmen made at home (figure 80).

Art glass sold for less than half the price of elaborate cut glass. It is likely that cut glass appealed more to conservative buyers (cut glass had always been the most expensive style and was therefore regarded as "the best"), whereas art glass was favored by less traditional buyers interested in something new and stylish. Both styles suited the cluttered, overdecorated Victorian interiors, however, and they remained widely popular throughout the last two decades of the 19th century.

The popularity of art glass was one of many American manifestations of the earlier English Aesthetic movement aimed at beautifying the contents of the home. Based on the social-reform views of John Ruskin, the movement was a reaction to a perceived deterioration of social values and the general quality of life due to increasing industrialization. Ruskin and his followers looked back to the craftsman, the guild, and the handmade object of the

75. The style of decoration on this Royal Flemish vase, said to have been developed in imitation of stained-glass windows, was patented by the Mount Washington Glass Company in 1889.

76. *Produced in imitation of porcelain, this Crown Milano cup and saucer set, about 1890–1895, was probably not meant to be used but to be preserved carefully as a keepsake. Crown Milano, Albertine, and Dresden were all names used by the Mount Washington Glass Company for their porcelainlike white glass with enameled decoration.*

78. *Most of the art glasses, such as this Burmese vase, produced by the Mount Washington Company are translucent, not transparent. They often resemble porcelain more than glass.*

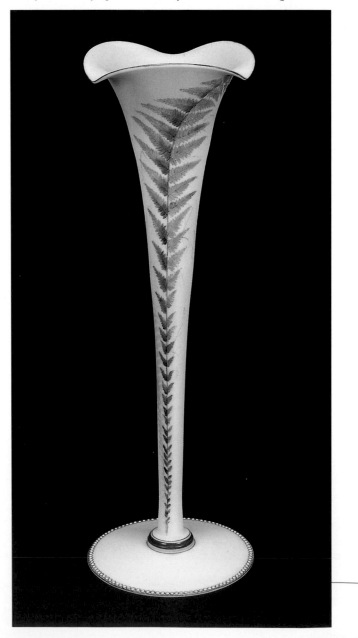

77. *Burmese glass was patented by the Mount Washington Glass Company in 1885. Its color was said to resemble a sunset in Burma. The yellow color of this Burmese lamp results from the use of uranium oxide and the pink comes from gold. The intensity and amount of pink were produced by reheating.*

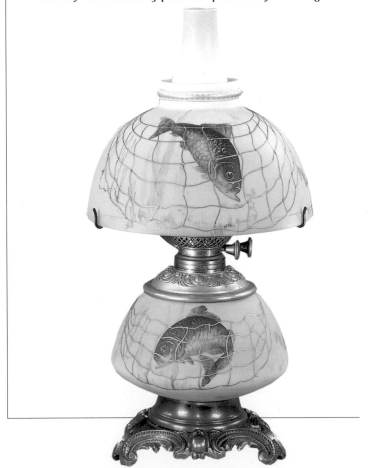

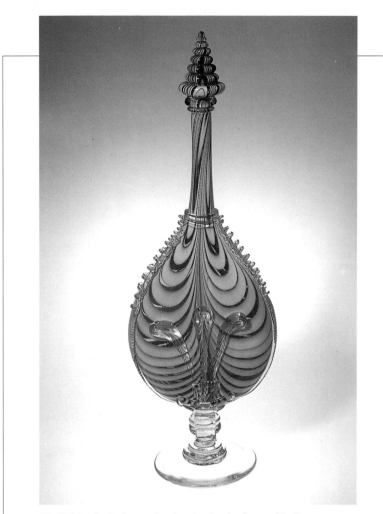

79. Whimsical, decorative bottles in the form of bellows were popular in American and English glasshouses during the last half of the 19th century. This example is one of the most elaborate known. It was made at the Mount Washington Glass Company, New Bedford, Massachusetts, and was blown by John Liddell, about 1885.

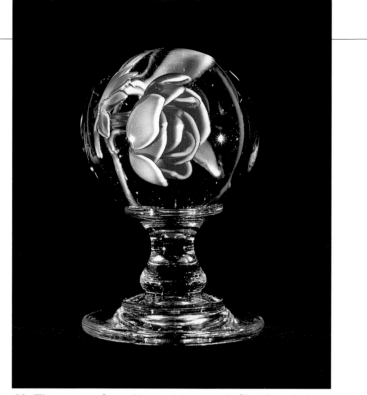

80. The rose was formed by applying a pad of bright red glass to the side of a colorless glass sphere. A "crimp" with curved metal fins arranged in concentric rings on a wooden handle was pushed against the red glass pad while it was molten, forcing the color inside the colorless ball. When the ball was reshaped, rounded, and covered with more colorless glass, the back of the rose was rounded and closed. A lampworked green stem and leaves were added behind the rose to complete the ensemble. Like most American paperweights with enclosed flowers, this was made by the glassblower on his own time with leftover glass. Ralph Barber is considered one of the most skillful American paperweight makers. Attributed to Whitall Tatum Company, Millville, New Jersey, c. 1905–1912.

medieval period as models for a superior way of living. These ideas, which evolved into the Arts and Crafts movement, had international repercussions and soon were transported to the rest of Europe and the United States.

One result of Ruskin's nostalgic look to the past was a renewed interest in the neglected medium of stained glass and its extension from exclusively re-ligious architecture to the secular. The style most admired was that of the 12th century, which was characterized by small areas of brilliant color bounded by heavy black lead lines. It was now applied to a figural style, derived from the English Pre-Raphaelite artists, by firms such as those of William Morris in England and William Willet (figure 87) in the United States.

6

Early 20th-Century Glass

81. This type of iridescent pressed glass is called "carnival glass" by American collectors. Much of it was given away as prizes at carnivals after it declined in popularity in the 1920s. It was very inexpensive when made; a punch set like this cost $4.25 in 1910.

Gradually, the international artistic style called Art Nouveau made elaborate art and cut glass seem fussy. People of discriminating taste began to prefer the simple flower-form vases of Louis Comfort Tiffany (figures 84 and 85) and his competitors to strongly colored art glass and complex, prickly cut glass. The fact that several Midwestern firms were producing pressed glass imitations of the colorful art glass also contributed to its decline. Milk white glass, marbleized glass, and iridescent pressed glass (figure 81) in several colors were made in quantity from 1890 to about 1920 in the factories of western Pennsylvania, Ohio, and West Virginia.

This Art Nouveau or *Jugendstil* style,

which enjoyed a brief burst of popularity on the Continent at the turn of the century, was less extreme and not as pervasive in the United States. Rather than incorporating the sensuous whiplash curve of the Belgian and French schools, the American interpretation clung steadfastly to its English Aesthetic roots, spiced with large doses of Oriental motifs. The architect Louis Sullivan typified the style in the intricate foliate ornamentation he designed for his buildings. The radical severity of the designs of Sullivan's employee Frank Lloyd Wright established a link between American architecture/design and the simplified geometry of the Vienna Secessionists.

Perhaps some of the most profound American contributions to the art of the period came in the medium of stained glass. John La Farge and Tiffany were skilled painters who had turned to interior design, believing, like their European counterparts, that the decorative arts could be raised to the level of fine art. Working separately but at approximately the same time during the 1870s, they directed their interest specifically to stained glass and the development of new types of glasses to incorporate into their designs. The conventional term "stained glass" is

82. The artist and designer Louis C. Tiffany, along with the painter John La Farge, pioneered the development of stained-glass windows that were markedly different from the medieval style of stained glass popular earlier in the century. Tiffany worked with his craftsmen to create new types of textured glasses, sometimes with iridescent surfaces. In his floral and landscape windows, the entire visual effect is rendered solely through layering, calligraphic lead lines, and the quality of the glass itself—no paint or enamel is used. With their new attitudes toward glass, Tiffany and La Farge revolutionized the medium. Their work was of high technical quality and expensive to produce. Windows such as this one decorated many upper-class American homes around the turn of the century.

83. Tiffany is said to have turned to lamps to use the leftover pieces from his stained-glass windows. In any case, the designs are often similar, and they were perfect for the new electric lamps, which provided a constant intensity of light. The cast-bronze base was designed and made by Tiffany Studios.

means available to make glass resembling water, sun-dappled foliage, or drapery folds. Both Tiffany and La Farge used the new glass in layers to create painterly impressions, often of idealized, illusionistic scenes from nature, in sharp contrast to the flat medieval-style imagery (figure 82). To further the effect of painting in light and color, the copper foil or lead line holding the pieces of glass together was varied in width to create the appearance of a brush line. Often, cast and cut glass jewels or smooth beach stones were incorporated into a window, intensifying its rich color and texture.

Of the two, Tiffany was ultimately to be more widely recognized due to his early commercial success and the wide distribution of his production. He came from an affluent family whose firm, Tiffany and Company, had gained renown in the mid-19th century for its fine metalwork and jewelry. As a young man, Louis Tiffany was privileged to travel extensively through Europe and North Africa, developing a taste for opulent furnishings and exotic motifs. In 1879, at age 31, he established an interior decorating firm, Louis C. Tiffany and Associated Artists. The four partners furnished the homes of wealthy New York society, Mark Twain's home in Hartford, Connecticut, and the presidential residence, the White House, in Washington, D.C.

It was in the course of supervising the design of everything from the carpets, tiles, and light fixtures to the textiles for these environments that Tiffany focused his own interest on glass. In 1886, he initiated the first of many reorganizations and corporate name changes when the firm was christened the Tiffany Glass Company. Without his partners, he was now free to devote his energies and resources completely to this material.

somewhat misleading for their medium because both Tiffany and La Farge were far more interested in producing effects from the color of the glass itself than in painting or staining it in the manner of their Gothic Revivalist contemporaries.

La Farge can be credited with developing the milky, striated, opalescent glass that revolutionized the medium by allowing artists a whole new range of effects. It was Tiffany, however, who urged his employees to stretch, roll, impress, and use any other

The fabrication of Tiffany's windows required considerable time and effort because each section of glass had to be selected for exactly the right effect, then cut from the larger slab. Imagination and artistic ability were required of the craftsman assembling the thousands of layered puzzle parts and envisioning them as a whole. When finished, the windows were unusually heavy and sometimes quite dense optically.

Close inspection of the most complex examples reveals areas of multiple layers of glass scattered throughout a single window, giving a contoured surface to the back side. A multitude of textured glasses were held together by the undulating lines of lead and copper foil that snaked from the surface to the inner depths of the glass, reappearing elsewhere. Usually, only Tiffany's religious windows, essentially mass-produced to satisfy a period of extensive church building, used paint to provide details on the figures.

Around 1899, Tiffany applied a simplified version of his window techniques to a much more marketable product—lampshades for Thomas Edison's newly invented incandescent bulb (figure 83). The illumination of electric lighting devices caused a warm, soft glow, permitting residents in many homes where a stained-glass window was not suitable or affordable to experience the effect of stained glass. The lamps, like the windows, were designed by numerous artists, most often in floral designs, but sometimes with abstract geometric or insect motifs. Though produced in large numbers, these lamps, like all of Tiffany's output, were of high quality and always expensive.

In the process of developing new glasses for the windows, Tiffany saw another potential area of ex-

84. Like the greatest Art Nouveau glassmaker Emile Gallé, Tiffany took his inspiration from the forms of nature. The theme of the flower was perfectly adapted to the flower-form vase, and Tiffany's floral forms were imitated by many other manufacturers in the United States and Europe. The blown glass from Tiffany's furnaces was one of the most important American contributions to the Art Nouveau style.

pression (and sales) in blown objects (figures 84–86). He established his own glasshouse in Corona, Long Island. Around 1893, he had patented a process for making iridescent glass whose multicolored, shimmering surface imitated the decaying outer skin of long-interred ancient glass. Tiffany's workers used this technique in the production of hand-blown decorative vessels and tableware as well as the flat glass required for the mosaics, windows, and lamps. Outside of several commissions done for the Parisian

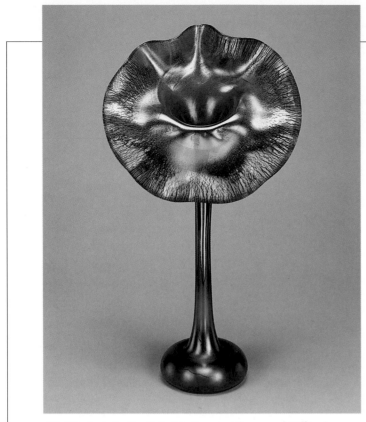

85. *The Jack-in-the-Pulpit is the most famous of Tiffany's forms. This example, made about 1912, was given its iridescent sheen by adding metallic salts to the glass batch, subjecting the molten form to a reducing flame, and spraying it with additional metallic salts. A wide variety of colors and hues could be obtained by this process, but the most popular were peacock blue and a shimmering gold.*

dealer Siegfried Bing to reproduce the designs of leading French artists, Tiffany's stained-glass windows could not truly be called Art Nouveau in style. Conversely, the flowing, organic quality of his blown glass placed it squarely within the parameters of European Art Nouveau.

The vessels often took the shape of graceful flowers with elongated stems such as the "Jack-in-the-Pulpit" (figure 85), and at times they imitated early Roman artifacts. The glass in which Tiffany himself took greatest pride was the most irregular in form, with bubbly, rough surfaces; he called this glass "Cypriot" and "Lava." It was reminiscent of molten rock and similar in appearance to Japanese *raku*-fired tea bowls. Tiffany patented the name "Favrile" in 1894 and used it generically to describe not only the glass but also many of the other objects produced by his company, such as jewelry, enamels, and pottery.

The fame of Tiffany's stained and blown glass business soon led to many imitators and rivals. In the United States, the Durand Art Glass Company, the A. Douglas Nash Corporation, the Quezal Art Glass & Decorating Company, and the Union Glass Company (responsible for "Kew Blas") produced work similar to Tiffany's. Other companies, such as Steuben Glass in America and Johann Loetz-Witwe

86. *Although today's admirer of Tiffany glass most often thinks of the flower-shaped vases with their brilliantly iridized surfaces, Tiffany himself considered his less obviously beautiful glass to be one of his greatest achievements. Only his finest work, such as this vase, would have been reserved for the great international exhibitions, and these objects were rarely sold. Tiffany was a shrewd publicist, and knew the importance of international recognition and of placement of his work in prominent museum collections of the day.*

of Bohemia, contested Tiffany's claim to the earliest exploitation of the iridization process.

Although Tiffany enjoyed international acclaim, was a noted exhibitor at the 1893 World's Columbian Exposition in Chicago, and received a gold medal at the 1900 Paris Exposition Universelle, the Art Nouveau style had long been abandoned in Europe and was fading out of fashion in the United States by the 1920s. Tiffany saw his life's work scorned by the public and the business floundering. In 1932, Tiffany Studios filed for bankruptcy; the following year, Louis Comfort Tiffany died.

87. William Willet (1869–1921) studied under John La Farge, but he was more interested in returning to a medieval style of stained glass than in using La Farge's glass innovations to create illusionistic impressions. Although designed in the 20th century, these two stained-glass windows, **Beatrice** *and* **Dante**, *are an extension of the English Pre-Raphaelite style popular in Europe 40 years earlier. The figures dominate the frame, with features of the face and hair reminiscent of the paintings by Dante Gabriel Rossetti and Edward Burne-Jones. The garments flow loosely around the figures, which stand within a framework of small areas of color. The literary subject suggests that these windows may have been designed for a public or home library. The inscriptions are from* **La Vita Nuova**, *translated by Dante Gabriel Rossetti.*

Left panel:

Even as the others mock, thou mockest me;
Not dreaming, noble lady, whence it is
That I am taken with strange semblances,
Seeing thy face that is so fair to see.

Right panel:

Whom now I mourn, no man shall learn from me
Save by the measure of these praises given.
Whoso deserves not heaven
May never hope to have her company.

The Willet Studios in Philadelphia, still in operation, have been a leader in making ecclesiastical windows since the founding of the company in 1898.

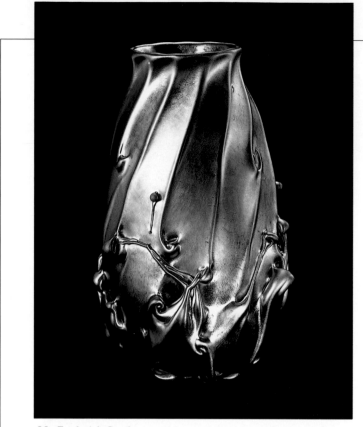

88. Frederick Carder was an experienced English glass designer when he came to Corning in 1904 to help found and manage Steuben Glass Works. He had spent years in England experimenting with an iridescent glass that he finally perfected around 1904. He called the effect "Aurene," a word he devised from the first three letters of aurum, *the Latin word for "gold," and with the last three letters of* schene, *the Middle English form of "sheen."*

Working almost concurrently with Tiffany from 1903 was another great glass innovator and designer, Frederick Carder. Born in England, Carder had been persuaded to leave the prestigious Stevens and Williams Company of Stourbridge to come to Corning, New York, with the aim of starting the Steuben Glass Company. Carder's glasshouse was to provide thousands of "blanks" (undecorated forms) needed by Corning's celebrated glass cutting firm, T. G. Hawkes and Company (figures 67 and 68).

Carder's experience and extensive knowledge of glassmaking technology immediately led him to expand his operation. The man who had been called upon by Peter Karl Fabergé to help manufacture tableware for the Russian imperial family was interested in much more than producing crystal blanks for cutting. By 1904, he was experimenting with colored glass, which he was soon forming into an astounding number of shapes using a multitude of techniques and colors. In that year, Carder registered the name "Aurene" for the iridescent glass he had perfected (figure 88). At first glance, his glass looks very similar to Tiffany's. Tiffany was so irritated that in 1913 he brought legal action against Carder for infringement of his patent; the suit was later withdrawn, without comment, before it went to court.

The discerning observer can detect the real difference between their work by studying the forms. Carder had been trained in the classical tradition, while Tiffany admired the French Impressionists. Where Tiffany's blown glass was often organic and spontaneous in feeling, Carder's designs mirrored the controlled symmetry of Greek pottery. Carder's genius resided in his chameleonlike ability to assimilate and adapt any style or technique that he saw—from Chinese cameo carving to French *pâte de verre* and Venetian *cristallo*.

7

Mid-Century Modernism

89. This vase was meant to be filled with water when it was used as the base for an electric table lamp. Carder's designs for Steuben glass in the 1920s were influenced by Venetian glass.

In 1918, the economic hardships of World War I forced the Hawkes family to sell Steuben to the Corning Glass Works, a larger firm that had been operating in Corning since 1868. That company retained Carder as managing director and later as art director. Until his removal from that position in 1932, Carder was responsible for virtually all of the artistic and technical innovation of Steuben.

Carder's stylistic flexibility allowed Steuben Glass, unlike Tiffany's company, to adapt to the ever-changing public taste. By the late 1920s many of Steuben's products and those of other factories exhibited the nuances of the popular Art Deco style (a style Carder personally detested), whose machined lines

90. *A console set consisted of a bowl and two or four candlesticks. Popular in the 1920s and 1930s, the set was intended to be placed on a table that stood against the wall of a dining room. The shape of the candlesticks and bowl in this set echoes earlier Venetian forms. The "Nubian Black" glass, popular in the 1920s, was very hard glass and difficult to engrave. Therefore, most of it was decorated by acid etching. The Sinclaire company of Corning was primarily a cutting and engraving firm. After World War I, a diminishing supply of quality blanks led H. P. Sinclaire to start his own glass factory in nearby Bath, New York.*

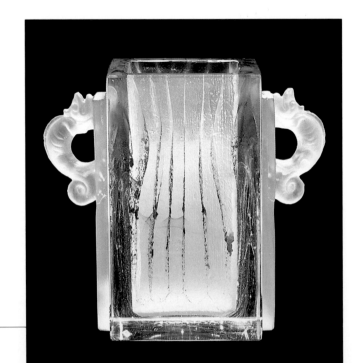

were considered more fashionable than the flowery Art Nouveau (figures 89 and 90).

Glass was an ideal vehicle for the streamlined aerodynamic shapes of modern furniture and applied arts. High-style interiors of the period were paneled with mirrors etched, sandblasted, or painted with decorative motifs. They were illuminated by the soft glow of heavy frosted glass fixtures and, in the most lavish settings, even graced with glass fountains.

Less affluent households used tableware and lighting pressed by fully automated machines. This glass was so inexpensive to produce that several glass factories managed to stave off bankruptcy during the Great Depression by making these wares. In 1926, the ribbon machine, an automatic blowing mechanism used primarily to manufacture light bulbs and (after 1939) Christmas tree ornaments, was developed by Corning Glass Works engineers. It proved so productive (2,000 bulbs a minute, nearly three million in a day) that the process was soon licensed to other glass companies (one was recently built near Lvov in the Ukrainian S.S.R.), revolutionizing that portion of the glass industry. The development of this machinery was the logical outcome of the indus-

91. *After Frederick Carder was replaced as manager of Steuben in 1932, he began to form glass objects in a small kiln he built in his office. He created a wide variety of sculpture and vessels using the lost wax (cire perdue) method. First, a wax vase was formed and encased in a ceramic material. When the ceramic mold was heated, the wax ran out—thus the name. Glass rods were arranged side by side in the mold; upon heating, they melted and filled the mold sections. The black streaks were caused by an impurity in the mold, but they give life to the form. This vase was made by Carder and his young assistant, Paul Gardner, who later became curator of glass and ceramics at the National Museum of History and Technology, Smithsonian Institution, Washington, D.C.*

92. *The influence of Swedish design on Steuben after 1933 is evident in the* Gazelle bowl. *The bodies of the engraved gazelles are almost sculptural, and the rhythmic design works well with the full, rounded bowl. The extreme clarity of Steuben's lead crystal is emphasized by the bowl's massiveness. The* Gazelle bowl *is widely regarded as a classic example of U. S. Art Deco design and a masterpiece of Steuben. This example may have been engraved by Joseph Libisch.*

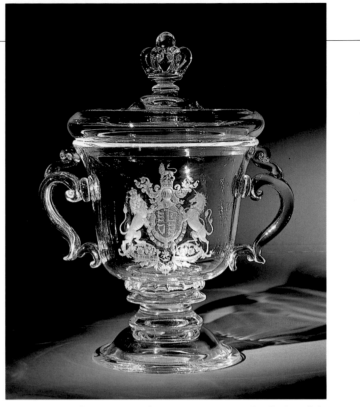

93. *The royal British coat of arms, encircled by the Order of the Garter, is engraved on one side of this valor cup. The urn was commissioned to show American support for the British in the early years of World War II. It was presented to the British War Relief Society in commemoration of the Battle of Britain. This replica, created at the same time as the presentation cup and given to the designer upon his retirement, was made by Jan Jansson and engraved by Joseph Libisch in 1941.*

trial improvements that had begun with the invention of the hand-operated pressing machine a century earlier.

In the 1930s and 1940s, many American designers looked to Scandinavia for inspiration. There, artists had been successfully integrated into industry by 1917, and worked closely with the craftsmen executing their designs. This cooperation between art and industry would serve as a model for the future. The spare functional elegance of Edvard Hald's and Simon Gate's transparent, engraved glasses for Or-

refors in Sweden influenced the design of much of the tableware produced by the leading American manufacturers, such as the Libbey and Fostoria glass companies (figure 94). Also, the geometric cutting and simple shapes championed by Josef Hoffmann and Koloman Moser in the Wiener Werkstätte—and further refined by its theoretical beneficiary, the Bauhaus—influenced American production. The unornamented designs of this higher-priced tableware could also be effectively produced in large numbers entirely, or in part, by machines.

94. In 1940, the Libbey Glass Company decided to produce a group of streamlined cut glass—the "Modern America" series. Unfortunately, World War II cut off lead supplies, and little of the glass was actually produced.

The Great Depression of the 1930s and the closing of almost all of the art glass companies producing colored glass prompted Steuben Glass to modify and modernize its product. In 1932, the young architect John Monteith Gates became managing director of Steuben, and Sidney Waugh was named designer. A new formula for a brilliant high-lead glass was developed, and the successful stylistic formula that has characterized Steuben for more than 50 years appeared almost overnight: colorless glass of the purest quality was hand-formed into simple, weighty shapes, often decorated with fine engraving, and then marketed in exclusive stores (figures 92, 93, and 99).

Outside of the manufacture of tableware and decorative items, glass was becoming increasingly prominent as a building material. The impending war brought many architects and designers of the German Bauhaus school, such as Walter Gropius and Mies van der Rohe, to the United States. Eventually, they changed the face of American cities with their glass-walled houses and skyscrapers.

During the years following 1945, the American glass industry became more mechanized, although scattered small factories concentrated in Ohio and West Virginia, as well as Steuben, maintained their handwork operations. The most avant-garde contemporary design continued its close relationship with European functionalism. Now, shapes exhibited a softer, biomorphic quality influenced by Surrealist painting and sculpture (figure 95).

In 1959, eight years after it first opened its doors, The Corning Museum of Glass organized an international survey of the best glass, called "Glass 1959." Of the 292 pieces selected for the exhibition, fewer than 50 were designed and created by the same person. In most of these instances, the artist worked in a factory atelier. The exhibition was the first opportunity in the West to study the results of the unique relationship between Czechoslovakian artists and industry, which had only been glimpsed at the 1958 Brussels exposition.

Though barely reflected in the inventory of "Glass 1959," the post–World War II period was a time of revitalization for handicrafts in the United States. Soldiers returning from the war received scholarships from the federal government to continue their education. Several used the opportunity to attend universities and schools where they studied the traditional fine arts such as painting and sculpture, as well as the crafts. In the process, they discovered new materials and sought out international folk crafts.

While the other craft media flourished, the age-old technical difficulties of working with glass caused it to lag behind in development. The strong tradition of glass technical schools in Europe, where students were trained in all the techniques of cold-working, had no equivalent in the United States. A person interested in learning to form glass had to seek knowledge outside the country or to learn by experimentation and the study of technical publications written for scientists and engineers.

Working molten glass then was almost impossible for the independent artist. Even Maurice Marinot, the French painter who, around 1911, was the first artist to choose glass as his preferred medium, had to rely on the facilities of a friend's factory to practice his art. When that factory closed in 1937, Marinot was forced to give up the blowing and etching of his sculptural vessels.

Jean Sala, a Catalonian working in France, was the

95. *This pitcher was included in "Glass 1959," an international exhibition of The Corning Museum of Glass. It was made about 1958 by the Viking Glass Company, founded in 1901 in New Martinsville, West Virginia. In recent years, many small American glass factories have closed due to financial difficulties. Viking, which closed in 1986, reopened in 1987 under new ownership. The curved lines and elongated pouring lip of this pitcher relate to the biomorphic style popular in America during the 1940s and 1950s.*

96. *Edris Eckhardt was trained as a ceramist, but around 1953, she decided to learn to form glass. According to a personal account, she managed to melt glass in her basement studio, and at times she rolled the glass into sheets using dampened wooden rolling pins. In* **Uriel,** *made in 1968, she used the lost wax method to make the mold, then filled the cavity with crushed glass in a technique similar to Frederick Carder's. She managed to execute her work without a scientific background or industrial resources. Eckhardt was one of the few artists exhibiting in "Glass 1959" to make glass sculpture outside the factory. In 1989, at the age of 79, she continued to sculpt in glass and metal.*

Kaziun used lamp- or flameworking to blow small artistic vessels and to form the intricate internal decorations of paperweights.

American artists choosing to use molten glass did so by kiln-forming. Edris Eckhardt, Maurice Heaton, Frances and Michael Higgins, and a handful of others were ingenious in their discovery of ways to make sculpture, murals, jewelry, vessels, and other utilitarian pieces in their studios. Placed in kilns used to fire ceramics, crushed glass could be fused in molds (figure 96), and sheet glass could be heated until pliable enough to "slump" over a form. Fired glass enamels and applied metals added decoration. All the artists were working independently, struggling without guidance to use the contrary material. Only Frederick Carder, then making his own cast works in a small kiln in his office (figure 91), had the technical knowledge to realize his complex ambitions in glass. By the late 1950s, the determination to create art from molten glass was brewing among several American artists dissatisfied with the restrictions of kiln-forming.

only artist melting and blowing glass in his own small studio in Paris during the 1930s and 1940s. Once he shut down his furnace around 1952, no artists were known to be blowing their own glass outside factories. A few Americans were fashioning small objects by manipulating slender glass tubes and rods over a gas-oxygen flame, but this technique was severely limited in its possibilities. John Burton and Charles

8

Studio Glassmaking

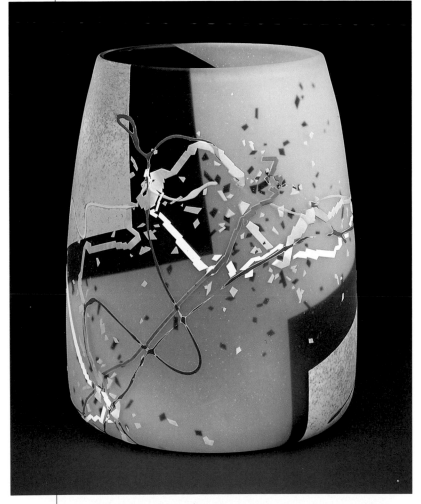

97. *The brilliant explosion of colored glass fragments that were applied to the glass while hot illustrates why* **Butterfly Finale** *(1983) by David White comes from a series named* **"Fireworks."**

Although many artists were experimenting (with largely disappointing results), one artist in particular was persistent in his search for a way to melt and blow glass himself. Harvey Littleton, born in Corning, New York, and the son of the Corning Glass Works' director of research, had been raised around glass factories and laboratories, and he had a lifelong acquaintance with his neighbor, Frederick Carder. Although he had been fascinated with glass since 1942, Littleton made ceramics his area of expertise, and by 1951 he was teaching at the University of Wisconsin. Searching for ways to blow glass in 1958, he traveled to Europe, where he met with Jean Sala and visited as many

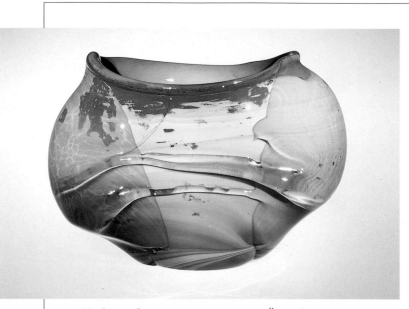

98. *Blown from stable, easily melted #475 fiberglass marbles, this bowl, made in 1965, shows the influences of Harvey Littleton's functional ceramic work as translated into glass. Nonetheless, such a simple work is a remarkable achievement, for it represents years of experimentation by an independent artist striving to melt and blow glass outside the factory. It also symbolizes the beginning of a new chapter in glass history—in which hot glass became widely available as a medium for artists.*

99. *The form of **Kisima** is that of an elephant's tusk, and the engraved decoration represents the animals at an African water hole. **Kisima** is a Swahili word for water hole. It was made at Steuben Glass, Inc., Corning, New York, and was designed by Donald Pollard (glass) and Bruce Moore (engraving) in 1960.*

glass factories as he could locate. It was not until he observed the small glasshouses on the island of Murano, near Venice, that he became convinced his dream of setting up a one-person glass operation was indeed possible.

Upon his return to Wisconsin, Littleton began looking for a location to hold a meeting with other artists interested in glass experimentation. He found that site at The Toledo Museum of Art, which offered to sponsor the event and provided a gardener's shed as a work space. The museum, holding a comprehensive collection of glass and located in a glassmaking community, was interested in encouraging advances in the medium. In March and June 1962, Littleton led two artists' workshops in kiln construction, glass composition and melting, casting, lampworking, finishing techniques, and, of course, glassblowing (figure 98).

Although Littleton was in charge, the first workshop was as much an education for the teacher as for the students. One of Littleton's acquaintances, Dominick Labino, glass scientist and engineer for the Johns-Manville Fiber Glass Corporation, volunteered technical advice and also donated materials for the experiment. (In 1965, Labino retired from his position in industry to devote the rest of his life to research and glassworking [figure 100].) After a disastrous first attempt to melt glass from a batch recipe of raw materials, the group began using Labino's #475 glass marbles, which he had developed for making fiberglass. Only then were they able to melt glass to a consistency suitable for their elementary efforts. A shed full of glass bubbles was soon the result. The excitement generated by the success of the two sessions ushered in a period of discovery and exploration—the "studio movement."

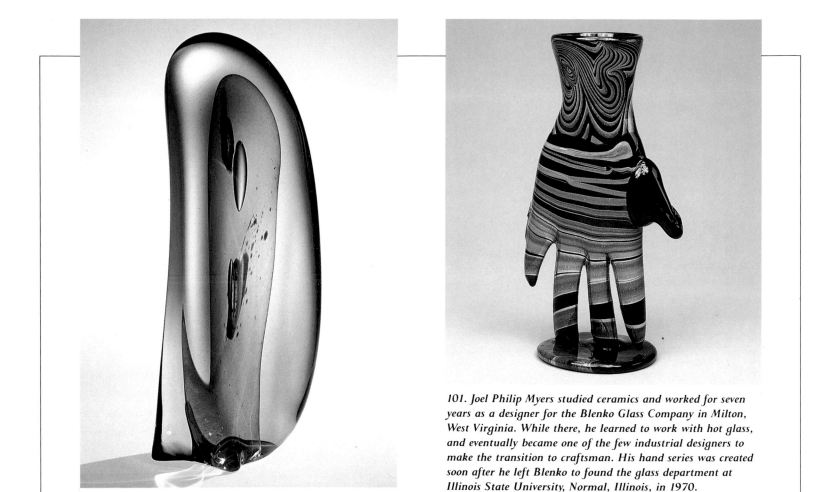

101. Joel Philip Myers studied ceramics and worked for seven years as a designer for the Blenko Glass Company in Milton, West Virginia. While there, he learned to work with hot glass, and eventually became one of the few industrial designers to make the transition to craftsman. His hand series was created soon after he left Blenko to found the glass department at Illinois State University, Normal, Illinois, in 1970.

100. Dominick Labino devoted much of his long career to the study and development of color in glass. His experimentation with the effects of metals on the glass mixture gave him great control over the difficult processes of obtaining a true ruby color by the addition of minute amounts of gold. This air sculpture, 1969, illustrates Labino's use of a simple, solid form to enhance the subtle coloration of the glass. Later, he fabricated large wall panels and freestanding sculpture using slabs of glass colored by the chemical interaction of different glass mixtures ladled over each other.

102. Mark Peiser studied music and worked as a product designer before traveling in 1967 to the Penland School of Handicrafts in North Carolina to learn about glass. He is one of the first American studio glass artists to follow Dominick Labino's lead in the study of glass chemistry by making his own glasses and colors. In 1970, he began the Fishbowl series of vessels, using opaque colors to create a spherical canvas for his literal imagery—in this case, a visual pun.

Immediately after the June workshop, Littleton traveled again to Europe. By chance, he encountered the work of Erwin Eisch, an artist making glass sculpture in his family's small factory in Frauenau, located in the Black Forest region of the Federal Republic of Germany. Eisch paid little heed to function, tradition, or even the craft of glassmaking. Instead, he was interested in glass as a sculptural medium—to be prodded, poked, engraved, or painted. In Eisch's work and attitude, Littleton saw a reaffirmation of his conviction regarding the potential of glass for sculpture. Through their friendship, close cooperation was established from the beginning between European and American artists.

In the fall of 1962, Littleton introduced glassmaking into the University of Wisconsin's art department curriculum. His students and other likeminded artists were soon giving workshops and initiating glassmaking courses in institutions of higher learning throughout the United States and eventually in other countries. The majority of these programs were incorporated into art departments

104. On May 4, 1970, at Kent State University in Kent, Ohio, four students demonstrating against the Vietnam War were killed by National Guard soldiers; 10 others were wounded. Henry Halem was head of that school's glass program, a position he retains today. The masked head depicted in this piece, made in 1972, symbolizes the Grand Jury of Portage County (town of Ravenna), which cleared the soldiers of charges of wrongdoing in the incident.

105. In the 1970s, Steuben began producing a series of glass jewelry. The cicada pendant was designed to be pressed into a mold, ensuring consistency of detail, reducing cost of manufacture, and allowing a greater number to be produced. The life cycle of the cicada has made it a symbol of resurrection and rebirth for artists since the Egyptian period.

106. While studying sculpture at the University of Wisconsin, Marvin Lipofsky joined one of Harvey Littleton's earliest classes in glass. In 1964, he initiated his own glass class at the University of California in Berkeley. Until 1987, he headed the glass program at the California College of Arts and Crafts in Oakland. This artist has always approached glass as a medium for his abstract forms, and like Erwin Eisch, he has at times found the "pretty" quality of the material a detraction. Some of Lipofsky's early pieces are covered with paint or textural materials that deny the translucency and reflection of the glass, forcing the viewer to heed the form instead. For the past several years, the artist has chosen to blow organic shapes into molds, then to alter them with cold-working techniques. Serie Fratelli Toso was made in Murano, Italy, in 1977–1978 by Lipofsky, assisted by Gianni Toso. The pieces from the 1980s accept, rather than challenge, the beauty of the material as part of the desired visual effect.

which, in the American system, were already integrated into the general universities. Glass courses were available not only to craft students but also to anyone studying in the university.

Art programs swelled in the 1960s and early 1970s as American universities were rocked by political events—specifically the movements for equal rights for minorities and women, and also the protest against American military involvement in Southeast Asia. Young people investigated alternatives to traditional values aimed only toward material reward. Many believed that they could obtain a simple, honest existence embodied in their idealized vision of a craftsman's life and work. Art became one vehicle for expressing their political and social beliefs (fig-

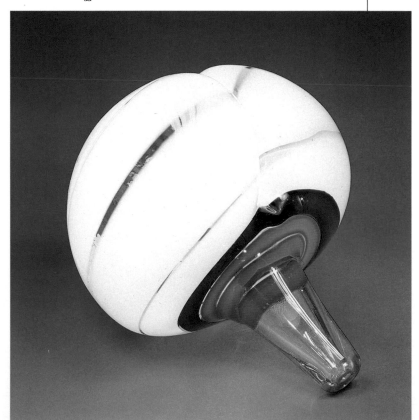

107. David R. Huchthausen had planned to study architecture at the University of Wisconsin, Wausau, where in 1970 he rebuilt an old furnace and taught himself to blow glass. Harvey Littleton was already working nearby in Madison, and in 1973 Huchthausen moved there to study glass. In the mid-1970s, he attracted attention with his multilayered blown and flame-worked "Fantasy Vessels." Huchthausen worked concurrently on a small number of architectural sculptures, such as Spider's Nest, whose shadows form an integral part of their visual effect. The use of blown sections laminated to cut pieces enabled the artist to produce a precise graphic form impossible to create by working with hot glass alone.

ures 103 and 104). Such a mixture of approaches and interests added to the rapid growth and diversity of artistic glassmaking.

The glass of the 1960s can be understood today as an experimental stage that was limited by technical understanding. One factor hindering the development of the movement was the earliest definition of studio glass as blown glass designed and made by the same artist working alone in a studio. Although the artist as craftsman was an important distinction, such a definition was limiting. Since then, the term has been continually redefined.

As artists gained technical skills, their bubbles and lumps of glass became vessels and sculpture (figure 98). These works were closely related in appearance to the ceramics that most artists had studied and produced previously. By the mid-1970s, artists tended to focus more on giving form to ideas than on mastering technical problems. The general homogeneity of the work decreased as diverse technical opportunities were realized. The Art Nouveau iridization process was rediscovered; molds gave control and consistency to blown forms; new adhesives and machines for cold-working permitted the production of shapes and sizes not possible with

108. This teapot, made in 1973, cannot hold or pour tea. In fact, though much of Richard Marquis's work refers back to a familiar functional form, it is sculpture commenting on the idea of a container rather than acting as a container itself. Marquis almost always makes his point using humor in a style that harkens back to its roots in Pop and "funk" art of the 1960s.

*109. Combining blown and cut elements, **Space Cup No. 7** (1976) is an early example in Michael Cohn's series (spanning a period of more than 14 years) exploring the evolution of a common cup to a futuristic machine.*

hot-working alone (figures 107 and 109); the availability of premixed colorants from Europe allowed a wide palette of compatible shades and hues. At times, the inherent beauty and "glassiness" of the material was completely negated by covering it with paint or other textural applications.

In addition to those artists wishing to master the glass craft and to make beautiful, well-designed, and useful objects, (figures 97, 105, 111, 112, 113, and 115), there were others who, in the spirit of Erwin Eisch, chose to create sculpture (figures 106, 114, and 116). This decision helped link glass and art in other media, but at times it inadvertently created a gap between those perceived as fine artists and those viewed, in a lesser role, as craftsmen.

Other artists worked in a literal whimsical style that was an offshoot of Pop art (figures 108 and 110). The humorous observations of everyday life were often translated into glass animals, food, or parts of the human body (figures 101 and 102). Cups sprouted legs; handles became arms. The influences of hallucinogenic art and science-fiction literature also added to the complexity of imagery and form.

*110. Robert Levin's vessels often include renderings of edible objects acting as stems or handles (an American favorite, the hamburger, is the most recent example). They invite comparisons with Claes Oldenburg's soft sculpture, but by the addition of the vessel element, Levin's goblets retain their functional potential. Oldenburg's work heavily influenced American ceramics of the 1960s. Like Richard Marquis's teapot, **A Cup with Appeal #2**, made in 1977, has close ties to this earlier style of "funk."*

111. *Sonja Blomdahl built her own studio in Seattle, Washington, where she creates banded vessels, attempting to perfect a beautiful, deceptively simple-looking object (1986).*

112. *The making of glass paperweights is an American tradition that predates the Studio Glass movement of the 1960s. First made by skilled gaffers in factories for their own amusement or as a company product, paperweights are produced today as works of art in the private studios of many glass artists. This* Purple Finch in the Snow *was made by Roland "Rick" Ayotte in Nashua, New Hampshire, in 1982.*

113. *Flora C. Mace and Joey Kirkpatrick are artists and glassblowers who have collaborated since 1979. They have also worked with Dale Chihuly for a number of years. In* Kally, *these artists used the technique of drawing an image in wire, filling it with colored glass, and then embedding the image in molten glass and further inflating the form. The technique lends an appearance somewhat like a watercolor painting.*

114. Harvey Littleton has employed glass in a wide variety of styles. At one point, he began heating and manipulating large bars of optical glass manufactured by Corning Glass Works. In **Pile Up** (1979), he has stacked the individual bars on top of one another over a metal cylinder.

115. Paul J. Stankard is one of the world's greatest paperweight makers and lampworkers. In his studio, he strives to reproduce accurately the delicate flora he studies and photographs during walks in the woods near his home. He developed a "Botanical" series to display the entire plant, with soil and roots, three-dimensionally. **Indian Pipe** (*Monotropa uniflora*), also known as corpse plant or ghostflower, grows in moist woodlands in warm and temperate areas of North America, in Japan, and in the Himalayas. The artist's fanciful root system includes "spirit people"—a whimsical touch to an unusual chlorophyll-less, saprophytic plant. This sculpture, **Indian Pipe** (1987), is part of the artist's "Cloistered Botanical Series, Tri-Level."

116. Dan Dailey heads the glass program at the Massachusetts College of Art, designs for Daum & Cie in Nancy, France, produces furniture and lighting, and fabricates blown vessels. Much of his work centers around cold-worked "Vitrolite" (an opaque sheet glass extensively used in architecture in the 1930s and 1940s) assembled in Art Deco—influenced motifs. **Café** demonstrates that there is a legitimate place for humor and wry social commentary in contemporary art.

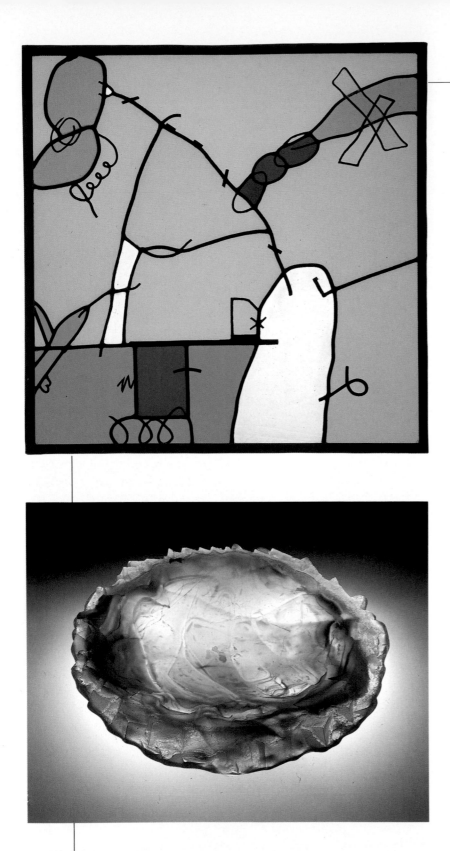

117. Under the influence of European artists, American stained glass began a transformation in the 1960s that revitalized the centuries-old medium. Abstract work such as Robert Kehlmann's **Composition XXXI**, *crafted in 1976, makes no attempt to imitate nature; instead, the inherent flatness of the glass and lead are acknowledged in the same way that modernist painters from Paul Cézanne to Frank Stella have recognized and accepted the inviolability of the picture plane.*

As European achievements, especially those of Czechoslovakian glassmakers, became more familiar, American artists explored the optical properties of glass (figures 119, 125, and 134). Casting, cutting, grinding, and polishing yielded prisms and lenses that refracted light and that magnified and distorted images. The viewer was afforded an opportunity to reflect on space and time captured in the cooled liquid. The metaphorical possibilities wrapped up in one material offered endless interpretations to artists using glass.

Stained glass was also influenced by European artistic tendencies. In the 1960s, German artists revolutionized and revitalized the medium, which had been in decline since the achievements of Tiffany and La Farge, and reintroduced it into architecture. In abstract geometric designs, the lead line became prominent again, and was relied upon for its graphic contribution—as important, in many cases, as the

118. Kent F. Ipsen is another early graduate of Harvey Littleton's program in Madison. Since that time, he has been a respected educator and artist in glass. Ipsen made his first baptismal font in 1975 for inclusion in the Vatican Museum's "Art in Religion" exhibition. In opposition to his previous blown work, this piece, formed by pouring molten glass into a mold, was unrestricted in scale and weight. Since 1975, casting and kiln-fusing have been this artist's principal techniques.

glass itself. On some occasions, the line was even structurally irrelevant and skitted across the surface of the glass like calligraphy (figure 117).

In the United States, flat glass became more three-dimensional, with projecting elements and applied nontraditional materials such as glitter, textiles, and junk jewelry. Some works become more pictorial, with enamels applied in an intimate, painterly style. Even the most basic features of stained glass, such as the leading, were sometimes eliminated. At other times, the light-transmitting ability of the glass was completely denied by obscuring the back and forcing the viewer to react to the light reflected from the front surface alone.

119. Using the technique of casting, Steven I. Weinberg explores positive and negative space as well as the optical effects encountered when viewing the enclosed topography through a mass of colorless glass.

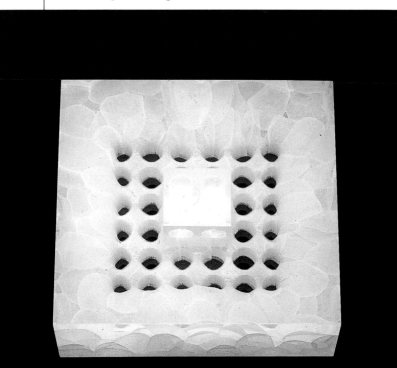

120. Peter Mollica's stained glass has more in common with painting than with architectural installations. In this untitled work created in 1977, the lead line has become a low-relief sculptural element, not simply a dark line. Mollica uses two techniques unusual in traditional stained glass. The first is "lost lead glazing," in which a piece of lead separating neighboring pieces of glass stops short, leaving the two edges of the glass bare, with a small space between. When those two bare edges are placed edge to edge with no leading, Mollica calls the process "butt glazing." Both of these techniques allow the artist to create a delicate and subtle drawing that is best studied within the intimate atmosphere of a gallery.

In the wake of enthusiasm for glass, many museums soon began to exhibit and collect the new glass. Commercial galleries were founded for its promotion, and they developed a new audience of collectors eager to buy. Such financial support, as well as the various governmental and private grants available in the 1970s, enabled some artists to live entirely on the income generated by their work. Like other artists, however, most of those working in glass have typically continued to depend on teaching or other positions for the majority of their income, or they have devoted a portion of their time to producing more commercially viable work.

The numbers of aspiring artists multiplied as glass programs proliferated, and they banded together.

122. Although Jay Musler is a skilled glassblower, most of his work does not depend on crafting the molten glass himself. Instead, he uses window glass or, in this case, commercially made glass, which he then modifies by sandblasting and painting. Musler often deals with dark subjects such as prison, loneliness, death, and the urban environment as in Cityscape, *made in 1981. In the words of the artist, "The colors and forms of these vessels express anger and alienation, as well as the threat of our existence on earth."*

121. Desiring to give his images more depth and detail and to make use of the interior volume of the vessel, Mark Peiser abandoned the opaque backgrounds he had used earlier (such works as Fishbowl, *figure 102), and in 1975 he began to "draw" within the walls of his vessels using the lampworking technique. The enclosed landscape images of his "Paperweight Vase" series were built up by applying glass canes heated by a torch between successive layers of colorless glass. The process is a difficult one, since all decorating and forming of the vessel must be completed while the glass is still molten. A single piece, such as* Wisteria Trees PWV 079, *might require the artist to work in front of the furnace for 6 to 18 hours.*

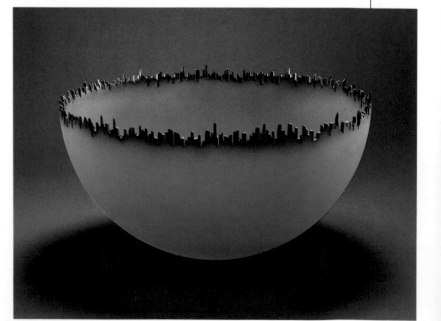

The Glass Art Society was organized in 1971 at the Penland School for Handicrafts in North Carolina for the benefit of those artists and other interested persons. The group's meetings have served as a valuable forum for communication and education in the glass community. In addition various international fraternal groups have been formed, including the Australian Association of Glass Artists, British Artists in Glass, Glass Art Association of Canada, and the Japan Glass Artcrafts Association.

In 1971, the artist Dale Chihuly and the businessman John Hauberg established the Pilchuck Glass Center (renamed the Pilchuck School in 1976 and the Pilchuck Glass School in 1986) on a tree farm near Seattle, Washington, as a school devoted ex-

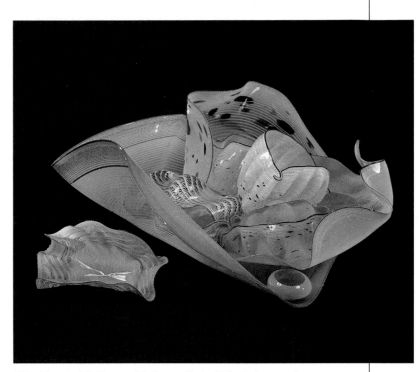

123. Doug Anderson is a leader in the international revival of pâte de verre (paste of glass), a technique developed in France around the turn of the century. The artist made molds, formed around real fish, which he then cast in wax and attached to a wax model of the bowl to create **Fish Bowl** *(1982). He then packed a refractory mold material around the wax, which, when dried, was heated, melting out the wax and leaving a cavity. The mold was filled with crushed, colored glasses that were fired slowly, then cooled over a period of days. Later, the mold was broken away, freeing the glass vessel.*

124. Along with Harvey Littleton, Dale Chihuly has made contributions to international contemporary glass through his art, his leadership as an educator (most prominently at the Pilchuck Glass School), and his promotion of glass as an artistic medium. Chihuly, who studied weaving, began in 1964 to incorporate glass rods into his work. His curiosity about the material led him to study with Littleton and later to work for a year at the Venini factory in Murano, Italy. Starting in the 1960s, Chihuly collaborated with other artists on a number of architectural projects and sculptural environments using glass, neon, and ice. In 1975, he began making a series of blown cylinders decorated with glass thread drawings that combined glass and the graphic designs of American Indian textiles. A short time later, in the storage vaults of a museum in the Pacific Northwest, he found some nested Indian baskets that were sagging under their weight. The image inspired him to create his "Pilchuck Basket" series, which gradually evolved into seashell forms. The thin blown pieces, which balance precariously, have grown larger, more complicated, and richer in color. In 1976, Chihuly lost the sight of one eye as the result of an automobile accident. Since that time, others have crafted the glass under his direction. This practice broadened the scope and potential of studio glass by encouraging other artists to work together. The Corning Museum of Glass **Macchia Sea Form Group** *was made in 1982 by Ben Moore and William Morris.*

125. Tom Patti was trained as an industrial designer rather than a glass craftsman. In the mid-1970s, he began to fuse stacks of industrial glasses, then to blow air pockets into the heated sandwiches to create vessels. Small in scale (Banded Bronze is one of his larger examples), the increasingly compact structures reflect Patti's study of architectural theory and his interest in the optical effects of glass. The artist has also created environmental plate-glass sculptures since the 1960s.

clusively to glassmaking (figure 124). Students have the opportunity to work there with an international faculty experienced in every facet of glassmaking and decorating. Instead of creating the atmosphere of a technical school, Pilchuck serves as a crucible of creativity where experimentation is encouraged—an approach that typifies the American educational approach to glass.

In an attempt to take a comprehensive look at the state of contemporary glass, as it had in 1959, The Corning Museum of Glass organized the exhibition "New Glass: A Worldwide Survey" in 1979. "New Glass" was circulated internationally, bringing the work to the attention of a wide audience. It provided an overview of the changes that had taken place in contemporary glass since the museum's earlier worldwide review, and it sparked interest among glassmakers and artists in many countries whose own traditions in glass art were either dormant or nonexistent (figures 120, 121, 126, and 132).

126. Dudley F. Giberson, Jr., is both an artist and a skilled designer and maker of glass studio equipment. He is well known for the glass bead jewelry he manufactures and the intricate murrini designs that are often part of his work. One of these designs is the animal motif decorating this piece called Two Kinds of Animals Finding Their Equilibrium in Nature (1978).

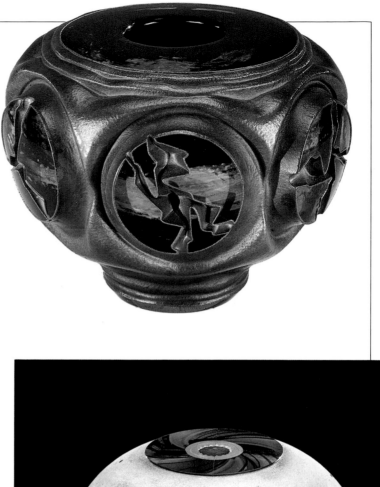

127. Michael Glancy teaches at the Rhode Island School of Design in Providence and maintains his own state-of-the-art studio. There, he produces massive vessels that are blown, deeply sandblasted, and then submerged in a carefully controlled electrolytic bath. As an electrical current passes through the liquid, the metal "grows" on the glass in a design predetermined by the artist. The rich ornament and weight of **Maelstrom** *(1981) suggest analogies to medieval gem cutting and metalwork.*

The diversity of the work was startling—the proportions of industrial and studio glass in "Glass 1959" were reversed. Now, studio work totaled 90 percent of the pieces selected and its influence on industrial production was noticeable. Steuben Glass, for example, had taken advantage of the purity of its material and its highly skilled cutters and engravers to execute sculpture designed and overseen by a select group of international artists. Steuben also showed glass designed by James Carpenter, a young artist recruited from the studio milieu.

The exhibition generated broader interest in new glass, and it raised anew many questions concerning the medium. Was it art, craft, design, applied art, decorative art, or something else? Where did it fit within the structure of public and private collections? Did it belong in art galleries and publications devoted to the fine arts? Was material alone a sufficient criterion on which to base an exhibit of such varied work? Could a vessel be sculpture? Was there,

128. Robert Clark Palusky's intricate globes (1986) require close study to reveal the surface subtleties. In other work, the artist creates cast figural sculpture that narrates personal incidents. Like many other glass artists, Palusky is a professor of art and maintains an independent studio for his private work.

129. Mary Ann "Toots" Zynsky lives in The Netherlands and the United States. Her friend Mathijs Teunissen Van Manen invented a machine that pulls glass into threads that Zynsky forms and fuses in a kiln. The artist calls this technique "filet-de-verre." In her earlier works, the threads were fragmented and matted together like a bird's nest. Her recent pieces focus on the pleasing symmetry of the lines laid side by side. Still reminiscent of a nest form, they are sometimes vibrantly colored, like the plumage of an exotic bird. The artist has designed a series for the Venini factory in Murano. She has also worked with the Ministry of Culture in Ghana to record the traditional music of that country.

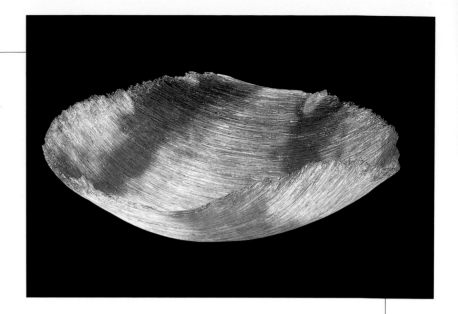

130. Like Toots Zynsky, Richard Meitner is an American who currently makes his home in Amsterdam. He is an independent artist and a teacher in the glass department of the Gerrit Rietveld Acadamie (the first Continental art school to offer instruction in hot glass, under the direction of Sybren Valkema, in the late 1960s). In his work, made in 1984, Meitner uses the structure of the vessel and enameled imagery to trick the eye of the viewer.

131. William Carlson heads the glass department at the University of Illinois in Champaign. He is an accomplished glassblower who is recognized today for his layered, laminated, cut, and inlaid constructions of glass and stone. "Contrapuntal" is defined as a contrasting or interweaving of elements. These angular pieces in this #75–64 Contrapuntal Series, created in 1985, demonstrate a kinship with Suprematist and Constructivist designs of pre- and postrevolutionary Russia.

132. *James R. Harmon is well known in the United States for the diversity of his work. In addition to blown-glass sculpture, he creates neon and mixed-media installations as well as lighting and tableware designs for limited-edition production.* 2011 CSDV *and* DV1504 *were created in 1977.*

133. *In the tradition of Frederick Carder's heavy, lost wax, cast forms, Karla Trinkley makes fused vessels that have evolved from a crustlike thinness to the rough monumentality of* Spoke *(1986). Her forms often seem to relate to cast bronzes from ancient civilizations, and they bear a patina suggesting age.*

134. *Paul Schulze retired in 1987 after serving as director of design for Steuben Glass for 26 years. He is a native New Yorker who employed the flawless quality of Steuben glass and the skills of its cutters and engravers to create this tribute,* New York, New York *(1984), to the "Big Apple"—New York City. The four corners are cut to depict, when viewed from the opposite faces, four famous skyscrapers in New York City: the twin towers of the World Trade Center, the Empire State Building, the Chrysler Building, and the Woolworth Building.*

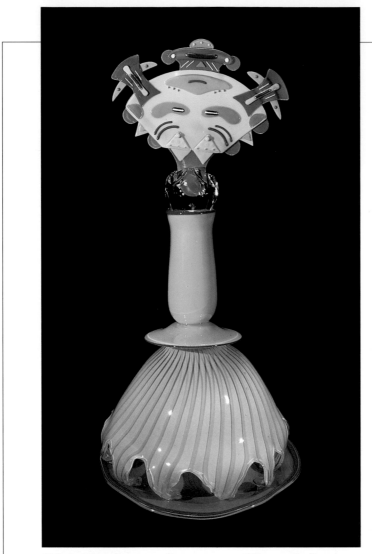

in fact, such a thing as glass art, a studio glass movement, or even a glass artist (figures 118, 122, 123, 127, 128, 129, 130, and 133)?

While curators, collectors, dealers, critics, and artists have attempted to resolve the debate, artists have continued to explore the apparently inexhaustible sculptural potential of glass—alone and in combination with other materials. As interest and accessibility have grown, so have the numbers of artists unconcerned with glass as a craft. Technically, there are still areas to conquer, but their number is rapidly

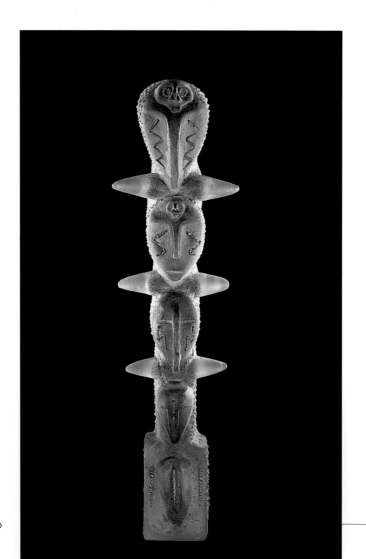

135. *In 1984, James van Deurzen was a fellow at the Creative Glass Center of America at Wheaton Village in Millville, New Jersey. This program invites artists to spend six months at the facility, where they are free to explore virtually every technique in glassmaking. Part of van Deurzen's production there included this anthropomorphic dancing* Japanese Headdress, *which combines kiln-formed and blown-glass elements.*

136. Totem, *like* Japanese Headdress, *was made by Mark Abildgaard during a fellowship at the Creative Glass Center of America in 1985. Its ritualistic form is meant to be viewed from two sides—through the crust of sand picked up from the mold surface and through the watery depths of the glass to the details trapped within.*

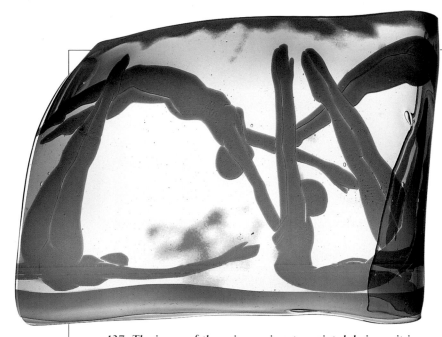

137. *The image of the swimmer is not a painted design—it is rendered in amber glass enclosed within layers of colorless glass. In this technique, known as "Graal," a bubble of colorless glass is covered with a colored layer. The partially shaped glass, or parison, is cooled and the design is etched, cut, or sandblasted, leaving only the colored design in relief. The glass is then reheated, covered with another layer of colorless glass, and blown, expanding the design. In this case, the glass was blown into a cylinder, then cut open and converted into its free-form shape in a kiln. This Swimmer was made by Stephen Dale Edwards in Kirkland, Washington, in 1983.*

diminishing. No longer is it necessary for artists to master difficult techniques in order to incorporate glass into their art. Glass has truly become an alternative for the sculptor who has no preconceptions about its use. Like all of today's art, it is impossible to organize art in glass into clear-cut classifications—a situation simultaneously healthy and disturbing (figures 131, 135, 136, 137, and 138).

In the years since 1962, the nature of studio glass has changed significantly. No longer is there the feeling of a "movement" in the earlier evangelical sense. Furthermore, a greatly increased interest in the material has eliminated the ability to identify a

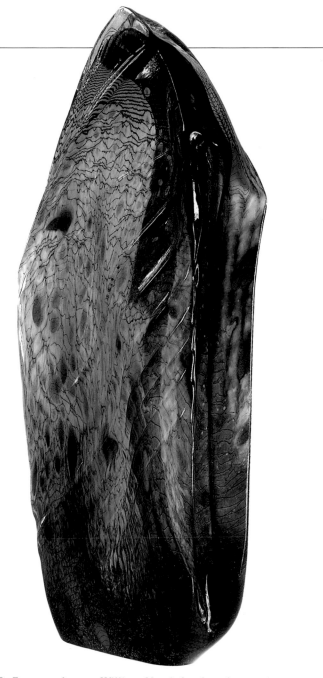

138. *For several years, William Morris has been known as a remarkable craftsman and the maker of much of Dale Chihuly's glass. He now uses his skills to create his own work. Morris's series of "standing stones" brings to mind comparisons with prehistoric stone configurations such as Stonehenge on England's Salisbury Plain. This untitled massive piece, created in 1982, was blown into a wooden mold that can be easily modified every time it is used.*

narrow group of "glass artists." Glass has ceased to be the young upstart in the art world, which has helped to blur divisions that artificially separated art and craft. The term "studio glass" remains convenient, but it is now more broadly defined. It includes the whole spectrum of hot and cold techniques used on both unique and multiple works. The idea of artist as craftsman revolutionized the appearance, use, and consideration of glass as an art form, but today artist-designed works are not necessarily made by the same person, or even by a person working alone. Artists in glass now accept the benefits of collaboration, and many have even returned to factory settings to realize projects impossible in small studios (figure 139). Many others continue to prefer the solitude of the private studio and to take pride and satisfaction in executing the work themselves.

When glass became accessible to artists in 1962, a new chapter in the history of glass was opened. One can find precedents in the work of Tiffany, La Farge, and other pioneers at the turn of the century. The history of American glass is a fascinating story, but it cannot be understood in a vacuum. To gain real insight into its significance, American glass must be viewed within the context of its precursors and resources. Its narrative is interwoven within the chronology of all glass and within the international history of art, design, and technology.

139. As a young sculptor, Howard Ben Tré first worked in bronze. For the past decade, he has used related casting techniques to create his sculpture in glass. Ben Tré's work reflects a longtime interest in architecture, and it makes references to archeological remains. The cracked greenish glass bears superficial patches of patinated copper. These details add to the impression of a failed machine first revered and then abandoned by industrialized society.

The Glass Artists

Mark Abildgaard (born San Francisco, Calif., 1957). San Francisco State University (B.A., 1979), University of Hawaii, Honolulu (M.F.A., 1983); Creative Glass Center of America, Wheaton Village, Millville, N.J. (fellowship, 1985). Lecturer and teaching assistant, University of Hawaii (1983); resident artist, Tokyo Glass Art Institute (1984); visiting artist, Sculpture Space, Utica, N.Y. (1985); lecturer, Hamilton College, Clinton, N.Y. (1986); started North Star Glass Company, Davis, Calif. (1986). Independent artist, living in Davis.

Doug Anderson (born Erie, Pa., 1952). Columbus College of Art and Design, Ohio (B.F.A., 1975); Rochester Institute of Technology, New York (M.F.A., 1980). Ohio Arts Council Fellowship Grant (1985); Rakow Commission, The Corning Museum of Glass (1986). Independent glass artist, living in Warsaw, Ohio.

Lloyd Atkins (born Brooklyn, N.Y., 1922). Pratt Institute, Brooklyn, N.Y. (B.I.D., 1953). Designer, Steuben Glass, New York City (1948–1984). Living in West Nyack, N.Y.

Roland ("Rick") Ayotte (born Nashua, N.H., 1944). Lowell Technological Institute, Massachusetts. He has 26 years' experience in the glass field. Independent artist making paperweights, living in Nashua.

Howard Ben Tré (born Brooklyn, N.Y., 1949). Portland State University, Oregon (B.S.A., 1978), Rhode Island School of Design, Providence (M.F.A., 1980). Rhode Island State Council on the Arts Grant (1979, 1984); National Endowment for the Arts Fellowship (1980, 1984); Change, Inc. Grant (1982); Rakow Commission, The Corning Museum of Glass (1987). Independent artist, living in Providence.

RIC MURRAY

Sonja Blomdahl (born Waltham, Mass., 1952). Massachusetts College of Art, Boston (B.F.A., 1974), Orrefors Glaskolan, Sweden (1976). Faculty glass instructor, Pilchuck School, Stanwood, Wash. (1985); the Appalachian Center for Crafts, Smithville, Tenn. (1986). Award winner, "Fragile Glass

'82," international competition, *Studio Glass Magazine* (1982); commissioned to make Washington State Governor's Art Awards (1985). National Endowment for the Arts Fellowship (1986). Built (1983) and operates her own glassblowing studio in Seattle, Wash. Independent artist, living in Seattle.

William Carlson (born Dover, Ohio, 1950). Art Students League, New York City (1970), Cleveland Institute of Art (B.F.A., 1973), New York State College of Ceramics, Alfred University (M.F.A., 1976). Head of the glass program, University of Illinois, Champaign (1976–   ). Fellowship, Cleveland Institute of Art (1973); National Endowment for the Arts Fellowship Grant (1981); Hokkaido Museum of Modern Art Prize, "World Glass Now '82" (1982). Independent artist, living in Urbana, Ill.

Dale Chihuly (born Tacoma, Wash., 1941). University of Washington, Seattle (1965); University of Wisconsin, Madison (M.S., 1967); Rhode Island School of Design, Providence (M.F.A., 1968). Head of glass department, Rhode Island School of Design (1969–1980); founded the Pilchuck Glass Center, Stanwood, Wash. (1971); artist in residence, Rhode Island School of Design (1980–   ). Rhode Island Governor's Art Award (1985); Governor's Award of Commendation, Washington (1985); National Endowment for the Arts Individual Artists Grant (1976); Fellow of the American Crafts Council (1986); honorary doctorates from the University of Puget Sound, Tacoma, Wash. (1986), and the Rhode Island School of Design (1986); Governor's Writers Award, Washington (1987). Independent artist, living in Seattle.

Michael Cohn (born Long Beach, Calif., 1949). University of California, Berkeley (B.A., 1972). Teaching and lectures/workshops at California College of Arts and Crafts, Oakland (summer 1973); California State University, Chico (1974, 1981), San Francisco (1974, 1978, 1982), and Long Beach (1981); Pilchuck School, Stanwood, Wash. (1978, 1984); and many others. National Endowment for the Arts Fellowship (1977–1978, 1984–1985). Independent artist, living in Emeryville, Calif.

Dan Dailey (born Philadelphia, Pa., 1947). Philadelphia College of Art (B.F.A., 1969), Rhode Island School of Design, Providence (M.F.A., 1972). Teaching fellowship in the glass program, Rhode Island School of Design (1972–1974); professor (1973–) and founder/director (1975–   ) of the glass program, Massachusetts College of Art, Boston; instructor, Pilchuck Glass Center, Stanwood, Wash. (1974–   ); instructor (1974–1986) and member of board of trustees (1983–   ), Haystack Mountain School

of Crafts, Deer Isle, Maine. Artist-designer for Cristallerie Daum (1976–   ); instructor, Center for Advanced Visual Studies, Massachusetts Institute of Technology, Cambridge (1975–1980); adviser, New York Experimental Glass Workshop (1979–   ). Fulbright-Hayes Fellowship (1972–1973); fellowship at Center for Advanced Visual Studies, M.I.T. (1975–1980); board member (1978–1982) and president (1980–1982) of the Glass Art Society. National Endowment for the Arts Fellowship (1979); National Endowment for the Arts Apprenticeship Program (1982); Massachusetts Council on the Arts Fellowship (1980, 1986). Independent artist, living in Amesbury, Mass.

Fritz Dreisbach (born Cleveland, Ohio, 1941). University of Iowa, Iowa City (M.A., 1965); University of Wisconsin, Madison (M.F.A., 1967). Teacher at numerous universities and glass centers, including Pilchuck Glass School, Stanwood, Wash. (1971–1982, 1984–1985, 1987–1988), Kent State University, Ohio (1986), Rhode Island School of Design, Providence (1972, 1976), Ohio University, Athens (1966, 1974–1975, 1977–1978), The Toledo Museum of Art, Ohio (1967–1970), and Chicago Art Institute (1970). Independent artist, working in Seattle, Wash.

Edris Eckhardt (born Cleveland, Ohio, 1910). Cleveland Art Institute, Ohio (Graduate, 1931; B.F.A., 1963). Head of the ceramics and sculpture division, Federal Art Project, Cleveland (1935–1942); faculty member, Cleveland Institute of Art (1932–1962), Western Reserve University, Cleveland (1947–1957), University of California, Berkeley (1962–1963), Cleveland College (1940–1956); and Notre Dame College (1950–1970). Guggenheim Award (1956, 1959); Louis Comfort Tiffany Foundation Fellowship (1956). Independent artist, living in Cleveland Heights, Ohio.

Stephen Dale Edwards (born Fort Worth, Tex., 1948). California College of Arts and Crafts, Oakland (B.F.A., 1972); University of Iowa, Iowa City (M.A., 1973; M.F.A., 1974). Instructor at Pilchuck School, Stanwood, Wash. (1980–1982, 1986), Pratt Fine Arts Center, Seattle, Wash. (1980–1986), Miasa Bunka Center, Nagano, Japan (1984). Independent artist, living in Kirkland, Wash.

Dudley F. Giberson, Jr. (born Alton Ill., 1942). Rhode Island School of Design, Providence (B.F.A., 1967). Participated in teaching workshops at Haystack Mountain School of Crafts, Deer Isle, Maine; Penland School of Crafts, North Carolina; Massachusetts College of Art, Boston; Rhode Island School of Design, Providence; Sheridan College of Art, Toronto, Canada. Author of *Joppa Glassworks Catalog of Facts and Knowledge*. Inventor and manufacturer of glass studio equipment and independent glass artist, living in Warner, N.H.

Michael Glancy (born Detroit, Mich., 1950). University of Denver, Colorado (B.F.A., 1973), Rhode Island School of Design, Providence (B.F.A., 1977; M.F.A., 1980). Teaching assistant, Pilchuck School, Stanwood, Wash. (1981); teaching assistant (1978–1980) and visiting artist (1982), at the Rhode Island School of Design, Providence; faculty member, Appalachian Center, Smithville, Tenn. (1984); visiting artist, Ohio State University, Columbus (1984); faculty member, Pilchuck School, (1982–1986); associate faculty member, Rhode Island School of Design (1982–1987). Independent artist, living in Rehoboth, Mass.

Henry Halem (born New York, N.Y., 1938). Rhode Island School of Design, Providence (B.F.A., 1960); George Washington University, Washington, D.C. (M.F.A., 1968); University of Wisconsin, Madison (postgraduate studies). First resident craftsman, Virginia Museum of Fine Arts, Richmond (1963–1964); ceramics instructor, Mary Washington College of University of Virginia, Fredericksburg (1965–1968); professor of art and director of glass studies, Kent State University, Ohio (1969–); director of graduate studies, School of Art, Kent State University (1982–1984); faculty member, Pilchuck School, Stanwood, Wash. (1982, 1983, 1986, 1987). Ohio Arts Council Fellowship (1979, 1982, 1986); research grants, Kent State University (1978, 1981); invited designer, "Focus West Virginia" (1976); invited artist, Interglass Symposium, Nový Bor, Czechoslovakia (1985). Independent artist, living in Kent, Ohio.

James R. Harmon (born Warsaw, N.Y., 1952). Rhode Island School of Design, Providence (B.F.A., 1975); Illinois State University, Normal (M.F.A., 1978). Instructor, Penland School of Crafts, North Carolina (1980); neon instructor, Pratt City Arts Center, Seattle, Wash. (1981); instructor, University of Hawaii, Honolulu (1980–1982); instructor, glass program, New York University, through the New York Experimental Glass Workshop (1985–); board of directors, Empire State Crafts Alliance (1985–); chairman, Artists Future Planning Commit-

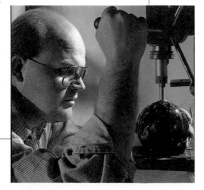

tee, New York Experimental Glass Workshop (1986–); instructor, Pilchuck School, Stanwood, Wash. (1987); instructor, Rhode Island School of Design, (1987); American Crafts Council Glass Award (1978); National Endowment for the Arts Master Fellowship (1979); Artist in Residence Fellowship, Art Park, Lewiston, N.Y. (1983); Creative Glass Center of America Fellowship (1984); fellowship, New York Experimental Glass Workshop (1985). Independent artist and designer, living in New York City.

David R. Huchthausen (born Wisconsin Rapids, Wis., 1951). University of Wisconsin, Wausau (A.A., 1973); University of Wisconsin, Madison (B.S.A., 1974); Illinois State University, Normal (M.F.A., 1977); University of Applied Arts, Vienna, Austria (1978). Curatorial and acquisitions consultant, Woodson Art Museum, Wausau, Wisconsin (1977–); associate professor of art, Tennessee Tech University (1980–). Newberry Award (1973); Woodson Foundation Grant (1973–1974); Elizabeth Stein Fellowship, Illinois State University (1976); Fulbright Research Scholarship (1977–1978); National Endowment for the Arts Fellowship (1982). Independent artist, living in Smithville, Tenn.

Kent F. Ipsen (born Milwaukee, Wis., 1933). University of Wisconsin, Milwaukee (B.S., 1961; M.S., 1964; M.F.A., 1965). Assistant professor (1965–1968) and founder of the glassworking department, Mankato State College, Minnesota; associate professor, School of the Art Institute of Chicago (1968–1973); associate professor and chairman, Department of Crafts (1973–1977), associate professor,

School of the Arts (1976–1980), professor (1980–), and founder of the glassworking department, Virginia Commonwealth University, Richmond. President, Illinois Craftsmen Council (1970–1972); state representative to American Crafts Council (1971–1972); National Endowment for the Arts Grant (1975); First Governor's Awards for the Arts (1979); Virginia Commonwealth University Grant in Aid (1980, 1985); Second Governor's Awards for the Arts (1985). Independent artist and instructor, living in Richmond, Va.

RICHARD SARGENT

Robert Kehlmann (born Brooklyn, N.Y., 1942). Antioch College, Yellow Springs, Ohio (B.A., 1963); University of California, Berkeley (M.A., 1966). Faculty member, Pilchuck School, Stanwood, Wash. (1978, 1980, 1985), and California College of Arts and Crafts, Oakland (1978–1980). Juror, *New Glass Review 4* (1983); member, board of directors, Glass Art Society (1980–1984); editor, *Glass Art Society Journal* (1981–1984); juror, Glass Art National, Downey Museum of Art, Downey, Calif. (1986), and Massachusetts Artists Fellowship program; Boston (1987). National Endowment for the Arts Fellowship (1977); Art Critic's Fellowship Grant (1978). Independent artist, living in Berkeley, Calif.

Joey Kirkpatrick (born Des Moines, Iowa, 1952). University of Iowa, Iowa City (B.F.A., 1975); Iowa State University, Ames (graduate work, glass, 1978–1979); Pilchuck School, Stanwood, Wash. (1979). Artist in Residence, Pilchuck Glass School (1980–1984); workshop, University of California at Los Angeles (1981); faculty, University of Illinois, Champaign (1981–1982). Independent artist, working with Flora C. Mace, living in Seattle, Wash.

Alan Klein (born New Haven, Conn., 1947). Southern Connecticut State University, New Haven (B.S., 1970); Rochester Institute of Technology, New York (M.F.A., 1974). Associate professor, Massachusetts College of Art, Boston (1980–1987); teaching posts at Toledo Museum of Art (1976), Bowling Green State University, Ohio (1976–1978), and Massachusetts College of Art, Boston (1980–1987). National Endowment for the Arts, Artist in Residence Grant (1975); New York State Grant, Art Park (1977–1979); Massachusetts Council for the Arts and Humanities, Fellow (1982). Independent artist and professor, living in Jamaica Plain, Mass.

Dominick Labino (born Clarion County, Pa., 1910; died 1987). Carnegie Institute of Technology, Pittsburgh (late 1920s). Owens-Illinois, Clarion, Pa. (1934–1946); vice president and research director, Johns-Manville Fiber Glass Corporation (1946–1965); adjunct professor, Bowling Green State University, Ohio. Honorary curator of glass, Toledo Museum of Art (1968–1987); Toledo Glass and Ceramic Award (1972); Fellow, American Ceramic Society (1973–1987); First Award, Ohio Arts Council (1971); Honorary Doctor of Fine Arts, Bowling Green State University (1970); Rakow Award for Excellence in the Art of Glass (1985). Independent glass artist who supplied critical technical information and the glass for both glassblowing workshops at The Toledo Museum of Art (1962) and inventor (more than 60 patents).

Robert Levin (born Baltimore, Md., 1948). Denison University, Granville, Ohio (B.F.A., 1971); Southern Illinois University, Carbondale (M.F.A., 1974); Penland School of Crafts, North Carolina. Teaching assistant, Pilchuck Glass Center, Stanwood, Wash. (1974, 1975); studio assistant, glass, Ohio University, Athens (1974–1975); instructor and resident glassblower at the Penland School (1975–1980). Chosen to create presentation objects for North Carolina Governor's Business Awards in Arts and Humanities (1980); North Carolina Arts Council Fellowship (1980). Independent artist, living in Burnsville, N.C.

Marvin Lipofsky (born Barrington, Ill., 1938). University of Illinois, Urbana (B.F.A., 1961), University of Wisconsin, Madison (M.S., M.F.A., 1964). Numerous guest instructor and visiting artist positions in the United States and abroad; instructor of design, University of Wisconsin, Madison (1964); assistant professor, Department of Design, University of California, Berkeley (1964–1972); professor and program head, California College of Arts and Crafts, Oakland (1967–1987). Top award, Milwaukee Designer-Craftsman Exhibition, Milwaukee Art Center, Wisconsin (1963); Merit Award, Craftsman U.S.A. '66, Museum of Contemporary Crafts, New York City (1966); Na-

tional Endowment for the Arts Fellowship (1974, 1976); Honorific Prize, Vicointer '83, First International Exhibition of Contemporary Glass, Valencia, Spain (1983). "California Living Treasure," Creative Arts League of Sacramento, Calif. (1985); Honorary Life Member, Glass Art Society (1986); Hokkaido Prefecture Overseas Cultural Fellowship, Bunka Shinko Kaigai Kouryu, Japan (1987). Independent artist, living in Berkeley, Calif.

Harvey Littleton (born Corning, N.Y., 1922). Brighton School of Art, England (1945), University of Michigan, Ann Arbor (B.D., 1947), Cranbrook Academy of Art, Bloomfield Hills, Mich. (M.F.A., 1951). Coordinator/instructor at both glassblowing workshops at The Toledo Museum of Art in Ohio (1962). Teaching positions at Ann Arbor Potter's Guild, Michigan (1947–1949), Toledo Museum of Art (1951–1977), and University of Wisconsin, Madison (1951–1977); chairman, Department of Art, University of Wisconsin (1964–1967, 1969–1971). Louis Comfort Tiffany Foundation Grant (1970–1971); National Endowment for the Arts Fellowship (1978–1979); professor emeritus, University of Wisconsin, Madison (1977); member, Academy of Fellows, American Crafts Council; honorary

member, National Council of Education in the Ceramic Arts; honorary life member, Glass Art Society; honorary Doctor of Fine Arts, Philadelphia College of Art (1982). Gold Medal, American Crafts Council (1983); Rakow Award for Excellence in the Art of Glass (1985); president, Board of Trustees, Penland School of Crafts, North Carolina; honorary member, American Ceramic Society (1986); North Carolina Award for Fine Arts (1987). Independent artist, living in Spruce Pine, N.C.

Flora C. Mace (born Exeter, N.H., 1949). Plymouth State College, New Hampshire (B.S., 1972), University of Utah, Salt Lake City (graduate work, glass, 1975), University of Illinois, Champaign (M.F.A., 1976). Teaching positions at Pilchuck School, Stanwood, Wash. (1981–1983, 1986), Haystack Mountain School of Crafts, Deer Isle, Maine (1985), and Nordisk Glas '85, Reykjavik, Iceland (1985). Independent artist, working with Joey Kirkpatrick, living in Seattle, Wash.

Richard Marquis (born Bumblebee, Ariz., 1945). University of California, Berkeley (B.A., 1967; M.A., 1969). Guest designer, Venini Fabrica, Venice. Teaching positions at the University of California, Berkeley; University of Washington, Seattle; San Francisco State University; and the University of California at Los Angeles. Independent artist, living in Freeland, Wash.

Richard Meitner (born Philadelphia, Pa., 1949). University of California, Berkeley (B.A., 1972); Rijksakademie v. Beeldende Kunsten, Amsterdam (1972–1975) The Netherlands; Gerrit Rietveld Academie, Amsterdam (Rijksdiploma, 1975). Freelance design work at the Royal Leerdam Glass factory; teacher, glass program, Gerrit Rietveld Academie (1980–   ). Independent artist, living in Amsterdam.

ROBERT SCHLINGEMANN

Peter Mollica (born Newton, Mass., 1941). Apprentice to Christy Rufo, Boston (1964–1968); traveled and studied stained-glass windows in England, France, Germany, and Denmark (1965, 1971, 1975); studied stained-glass design in England and Germany with Ludwig Schaffrath (1975). Author of *Stained Glass Primer* (1971; vol. 2, 1977; Japanese trans., 1981); several teaching posts, guest lectures, and workshops in the United States and Japan. Merit Award, Japan Stained Glass Design Competition (1979). Independent artist, living in Oakland, Calif.

William Morris (born Carmel, Calif., 1957). California State University, Chico; Central Washington University, Ellensburg; Pilchuck Glass Center, Stanwood, Wash. Teaching at Pilchuck School (1979–   ), Appalachian Center for Crafts, Smithville, Tenn. (1987), and at numerous craft schools, academies, and workshops. Independent artist, living in Stanwood, Wash.

Jay Musler (born Sacramento, Calif., 1949). California College of Arts and Crafts, Oakland (1968–1971). Instructor and guest lecturer at numerous universities. National Endowment for the Arts Fellowship (1982–1983); Honorary Prize, "World Glass Now '82," Hokkaido Museum of Modern Art, Sapporo, Japan. Independent artist, living in Berkeley, Calif.

Joel Philip Myers (born Paterson, N.J., 1934). Parsons School of Design, New York City (1954); ceramic design with Richard Kjaergaard, Kunsthaandvaerkerskolen, Copenhagen, Denmark (1957–1958); New York State College of Ceramics, Alfred University (B.F.A., M.F.A., 1963). Director of design, Blenko Glass Company, West Virginia (1963–1970); Professor of Art-Glass/ Ceramics, Illinois State University, Normal (1970–   ); participant, panelist, and demonstrator, International Glass Symposium, Museum Bellerive, Zurich (1972); member,

board of directors (1974–1978, 1982–1986), and president (1975–1976) of the Glass Art Society; National Endowment for the Arts Craftsman's Fellowships (1976–1984); Fellow, American Crafts Council (1980). Independent artist and educator, living in Bloomington, Ill.

Robert Clark Palusky (born Duluth, Minn., 1942). University of Wisconsin, Superior (B.F.A., 1967); Rochester Institute of Technology, New York (M.F.A., 1969). Assistant professor of ceramics (1969–1977) and associate professor of art (1977–   ), Hamilton College, Clinton, N.Y. Huber Grant (1971–1974); Mellon Foundation Research Grant (1973–1975, 1978); research grant (1982); research fellowship to study the glass collection in the Victoria and Albert Museum, London (1984). Independent artist, living in Deansboro, N.Y.

Thomas Patti (born Pittsfield, Mass., 1943). Pratt Institute, Brooklyn, N.Y. (B.I.D., 1967; M.I.D., 1969); New School for Social Research, New York City (1969). Consultant, American Federation of the Arts, New York City (1968–1969); instructor, Berkshire Community College, Pittsfield, Mass. (1970–1977); director, Savoy Art School, Massachusetts (1973–1979). National Endowment for the Arts Fellowship (1979); Massachusetts Foundation on the Arts Fellowship (1981); First Prize, "Freies Glas, Glaskunst '81," Kassel, Federal Republic of Germany (1981). Independent artist, living in Plainfield, Mass.

Mark Peiser (born Chicago, Ill., 1938). Purdue University, Lafayette, Ind.; Illinois Institute of Technology, Chicago; School of Music, DePaul University, Chicago. Numerous teaching positions, including Penland School of Crafts, North Carolina (1969–1970, 1972, 1979, 1985), The Toledo Museum of Art, Ohio (1973), Alfred University, New York (1974), Pilchuck Glass Center, Stanwood, Wash. (1975), School for American Craftsmen, Rochester Institute of Technology, New York (1976–1977), and Haystack Mountain School of Crafts, Deer Isle, Maine (1982). Tiffany Foundation Grant; National Endowment for the Arts Fellowship. Independent artist, living in Penland, N.C.

Donald Pollard (born Bronxville, N.Y., 1924). Rhode Island School of Design, Providence (B.F.A., 1949); trainee, silver design program, Institute of Contemporary Art, Boston (1949); architectural theater designer with Michael D'Angelis, Rochester, N.Y. (1950). Designer, Steuben Glass, New York City (1950–1981); free-lance industrial designer (1950–   ), living in Myrtle Beach, S.C.

Paul Schulze (born New York, N.Y., 1934) Parsons School of Design and New York University, New York City (B.S., 1960). Instructor, Parsons School of Design (1961–1969); guest lecturer, Rhode Island School of Design, Providence (1970–1983), Rochester Institute of Technology, New York (1987), Pilchuck School, Stanwood, Wash. (1982); designer (1961–1987) and director of design (1970–1987) for Steuben Glass, Corning, N.Y. Independent designer, living in New Suffolk, N.Y.

Paul J. Stankard (born Attleboro, Mass., 1943). Salem Technical Institute, New Jersey (Scientific Glassblowing Technology Diploma, 1963). Manager, Scientific Glassblowing Department, Rohm and Haas (1963–1972); workshops on lampworking, Kent State University, Ohio (1986), and Penland School of Crafts, North Carolina (1986, 1987). Commissions for presentation paperweights for board chairman of Mobil Oil Corporation, prime minister of New Zealand from Mobil Oil Corporation, and Deng Xiaoting of China by U.S. Ambassador John M. Cabot; Outdoor Club of South Jersey, Award for Artistic Efforts in Immortalizing the Beauty of the Flowers of the Pine Barrens (1985); New Jersey State Council of the Arts Grant; executive board member, Creative Glass Center of America. Independent artist, living in Mantua, N.J.

Karla Trinkley (born Yardley, Pa., 1956). Bucks County Community College, Newton, Pa. (1974–1976); Tyler School of Art, Elkins Park, Pa. (B.F.A., 1979); Rhode Island School of Design, Providence (M.F.A., 1981). Guest lecturer, New York Experimental Glass Workshop (1982), Tyler School of Art (1982, 1984), and Rochester Institute of Technology, New York (1986). Pennsylvania Council of the Arts Fellowship (1984); Asahi Shimbun Award, Hokkaido Museum of Modern Art, Sapporo, Japan (1985); National Endowment for the Arts Grant (1986). Independent artist, living in Boyertown, Pa.

James van Deurzen (born De Pere, Wis., 1952). University of Wisconsin, Madison (B.A., B.S., 1980; M.A., 1982; M.F.A., 1983). Teaching assistant, Pilchuck School, Stanwood, Wash. (1983); Creative Glass Center of America, Wheaton Village, Millville, N.J. (1984); prize winner, The Glass Gallery, Capital Glass Invitational, Washington, D.C. (1984). Independent artist, living in Mazomanie, Wis.

Steven I. Weinberg (born New York, N.Y., 1954). New York State College of Ceramics, Alfred University (B.F.A., 1976); Rhode Island School of Design, Providence (M.F.A., 1979). Young Americans Award, American Craft Council (1978); National Endowment for the Arts Fellowship (1978, 1984); third prize, World Glass Now, Hokkaido Museum of Modern Art, Sapporo, Japan (1986). Independent artist, living in Pawtucket, R.I.

David White (born Ridley Park, Pa., 1954). College of Architecture, Clemson University, South Carolina (1972–1975); College of Fine Arts, Illinois State University, Normal (B.S., 1977; postgraduate work, 1979). Graduate teaching assistant, Tennessee Technological University, Appalachian Center for Crafts, Smithville, Tenn. (1980–1984); studio artist (1984–); exhibitions preparator, Memphis Brooks Museum of Art, Memphis, Tenn. (1987–). Independent artist, living in Memphis, Tenn.

Mary Ann "Toots" Zynsky (born Boston, Mass., 1951). Haystack Mountain School of Crafts, Deer Isle, Maine (1970); Pilchuck Glass Center, Stanwood, Wash. (1971–1973); Rhode Island School of Design, Providence (B.F.A., 1973; Advanced Glass Program, 1979). Assisted Dale Chihuly (1971–1973) and Dan Dailey (1980) at Pilchuck; assistant director, New York Experimental Glass Workshop (1980–1983) and Haystack Mountain School of Crafts (1982); faculty member, crafts program, Parsons School of Design, New York City (1981–1982); department head, hot glass program, New York Experimental Glass Workshop (1981–1982); artist in residence, Pilchuck School (1982).  New York State Council on the Arts Artists in Residence Grant (1981–1982); National Endowment for the Arts Fellowship (1982); research grant, Stichting Klankschap Foundation, Amsterdam, The Netherlands (1984); Visual Arts Fellowship, National Endowment for the Arts (1986). Independent artist, living in Amsterdam.

Illustrations

1. Bottle
Wistarburgh Glassworks, near Alloway, N.J., c. 1745–1755. H. 23.5 cm. Transparent light green nonlead glass, blown, applied seal impressed "RW." The Corning Museum of Glass (86.4.196, gift of Miss Elizabeth Wistar).

2. Mug
Probably southern New Jersey, c. 1760–1810. H. 15.7 cm. Light green nonlead glass, blown, with spiral threading. The Corning Museum of Glass (68.4.6).

3. Candlestick
Possibly Wistarburgh Glassworks, near Alloway, N.J., c. 1739–1776. H. 18.7 cm. Transparent amethyst nonlead glass, blown and pattern-molded in a 22-rib mold. The Corning Museum of Glass (80.4.60).

4. Pocket bottle
Attributed to the American Flint Glass Manufactory, Manheim, Pa., c. 1765–1774. H. 13.3 cm. Deep amethyst nonlead glass, blown and pattern-molded in a "diamond daisy" decoration. The Corning Museum of Glass (50.4.22).

5. Covered sugar bowl
Attributed to the American Flint Glass Manufactory, Manheim, Pa., c. 1769–1774. H. 16.4 cm. Transparent dark blue lead glass, blown and pattern-molded in an overall diamond design (16 diamonds in a horizontal row). The Toledo Museum of Art (17.266).

6. Goblet
New Bremen Glassmanufactory, near Frederick, Md., dated 1792. H. 20.1 cm. Colorless (strong grayish tan tint) nonlead glass, blown, wheel-engraved name "G. F. Mauerhoff" within a Rococo scrollwork cartouche, inscribed on the reverse "New Bremen, State of Maryland. Frederik County. 1792." The Toledo Museum of Art (61.2).

7. Tumbler
New Bremen Glassmanufactory, near Frederick, Md., c. 1790–1795 (possibly 1792). H. 20.1 cm. Colorless nonlead glass, blown, with engraved initials "GMR" in a Rococo scrollwork cartouche; on the reverse, a naive country landscape with house, stylized trees and birds. The Corning Museum of Glass (55.4.281).

8. Pocket bottle
Probably New England, c. 1790–1810. H. 12.7 cm. Transparent olive green nonlead glass, blown and pattern-molded with intersecting vertical and spiral ribbing. The Corning Museum of Glass (55.4.262).

9. Footed bowl
Probably New England, c. 1790–1810. H. 8.5 cm. Transparent olive green nonlead glass, blown, trailed threading on the rim, applied circular foot. The Corning Museum of Glass (55.4.102).

10. Goblet
New Geneva Glass Works, New Geneva, Pa., c. 1798. H. 23.5 cm. Transparent green nonlead glass, blown; the hollow ball knop in the stem contains a silver medal from the College of Geneva, Switzerland. The Corning Museum of Glass (79.4.329, bequest of Jerome Strauss).

11. Footed bowl
Attributed to New Geneva Glass Works, New Geneva, Pa., c. 1798–1819. H. 14.3 cm. Transparent pale green nonlead glass, blown, molded spiral ribbing (24 ribs), applied foot with petal-shaped rim. The Corning Museum of Glass (55.4.99).

12. Goblet
Probably Marlboro Street Glass Works, Keene, N.H., c. 1820–1840. H. 17.4 cm. Olive green nonlead glass, blown. The Toledo Museum of Art (59.94).

13. Bowl and pitcher
Saratoga (Mountain) Glass Works, Mount Pleasant, N.Y., c. 1844–1865. H. (bowl) 16.8 cm., (pitcher) 21.8 cm. Transparent brilliant aquamarine nonlead glass, blown, with threading and superimposed gathers of glass drawn into stylized curved lily pads. The Corning Museum of Glass (50.4.447).

14. Vase
Probably New York, possibly southern New Jersey, c. 1835–1860. H. 22.7 cm. Transparent aquamarine nonlead glass, blown, trailed threading. The Toledo Museum of Art (48.46).

15. Vase
Probably southern New Jersey, c. 1849–1860. H. 23.4 cm. Transparent pale greenish low-lead glass with opaque white looping, superimposed deep amber glass, blown. The Toledo Museum of Art (48.49).

16. Mug
Probably southern New Jersey, c. 1860–1870. H. 15.3 cm. Transparent aquamarine and opaque white nonlead glass, blown; trailed and tooled threading. The Corning Museum of Glass (79.4.339, gift of The Ruth Bryan Strauss Memorial Foundation).

17. Gemel bottle
Eastern United States, c. 1830–1860. H. 21.1 cm. Colorless nonlead glass, blown, with opaque white trailed threading pulled into a chevron pattern. The Toledo Museum of Art (20.16).

18. Tumbler
Bakewell, Page & Bakewell, Pittsburgh, Pa., c. 1824. Sulphide

portrait of President Andrew Jackson in base. H. 8.4 cm. Colorless lead glass, blown, cut; molded white sulphide encased in the bottom. The Corning Museum of Glass (55.4.273).

19. **Celery vase**
Bakewell, Page & Bakewell, Pittsburgh, Pa., 1829. H. 25.8 cm. Colorless lead glass, blown, cut; engraved with a version of the Great Seal of the United States. The Corning Museum of Glass (79.4.6).

20. **Decanter and stopper**
Birmingham Glass Works, Pittsburgh, Pa., c. 1813. OH. 27.9 cm. Colorless lead glass, blown, copper-wheel engraved; pressed stopper (replaced, but appropriate type). The Corning Museum of Glass (55.4.44).

21. **Candlestick**
United States, probably Pittsburgh, Pa., c. 1840–1860. H. 31.5 cm. Colorless lead glass, blown and pattern-molded (pillar-molded) in an 8-rib mold. The Corning Museum of Glass (55.4.187).

22. **Compote**
Probably Pittsburgh, Pa., c. 1840–1860. H. 18.1 cm. Transparent amethyst lead glass, blown and pattern-molded (pillar-molded) in an 8-rib mold, applied solid stem and foot. The Toledo Museum of Art (87.40).

23. **Covered sugar bowl and cream jug**
White Glass Works, Zanesville, Ohio, c. 1815–1830. H. (bowl) 16.8 cm., (jug) 12.7 cm. Transparent sapphire blue nonlead glass, blown and pattern-molded in a 10-diamond mold. The Corning Museum of Glass (55.4.68; 55.4.74).

24. **Pitcher**
Probably Pittsburgh, Pa., c. 1840–1860. H. 21.5 cm. Transparent light violet lead glass, blown and pattern-molded (pillar-molded) in an 8-rib mold, applied hollow handle. The Toledo Museum of Art (84.27).

25. **Pitcher**
Possibly Sweeney's Glass Works, Wheeling, W.V., c. 1830–1850. H. 21.3 cm. Colorless lead glass, blown, cut. The Toledo Museum of Art (12.1383).

26. **Flask**
White Glass Works, Zanesville, Ohio, c. 1815–1830. H. 22.6 cm. Transparent golden amber nonlead glass, blown and pattern-molded with 24 intersecting vertical and spiral ribs. The Corning Museum of Glass (50.4.113).

27. **Bottle**
Probably Zanesville, Ohio, c. 1835–1850. H. 20.5 cm. Transparent cornflower blue glass, blown and with pattern-molded spiral ribbing in a 24-rib mold. The Toledo Museum of Art (59.67).

28. **Bank**
Probably Midwest, c. 1840–1845. H. 22.0 cm. Transparent pale amethyst (with aquamarine striations) nonlead glass, blown and pattern-molded with spiral ribbing, pincered trailings. The Corning Museum of Glass (66.4.51).

29. **Covered sugar bowl**
South Boston Flint Glass Works, South Boston, Mass., c. 1813–1829. OH. 23.8 cm. Colorless lead glass, blown; the hollow ball knop in the stem contains a loose Irish silver tenpence bank token dated 1813. The Corning Museum of Glass (73.4.116, gift of Dr. Malcolm Johnston).

30. **Covered sugar bowl**
New England Glass Company, East Cambridge, Mass., c. 1830–1840. H. 25.2 cm. Colorless lead glass, blown, spiral ribbing on superimposed gathers, trailed threading. The Toledo Museum of Art (53.75).

31. **Solar lamp**
New England Glass Company, East Cambridge, Mass., c. 1846. OH. 67.8 cm. Red and opalescent white lead glass, blown, overlaid, cut, enameled, gilded; colorless lead glass shade, blown, cut; brass and marble mounts. The Corning Museum of Glass (79.4.1).

32. **Whale oil lamp**
New England, c. 1813–1830. H. 19.3 cm. Colorless lead glass, blown, trailed pincered bands. The Corning Museum of Glass (72.4.52, gift of Preston Bassett).

33. **Vase**
New England, probably Boston area, c. 1825–1850. H. 19.1 cm. Transparent emerald green lead glass, blown and pattern-molded (12 rounded panels on the lower half). The Corning Museum of Glass (56.4.6).

34. **Lamp**
New England, c. 1830–1840. H. 43.2 cm. Colorless lead glass, blown, pressed, cut; brass collar. The Corning Museum of Glass (66.4.39, gift of Mrs. Jason Westerfield).

35. **Bowl**
Jersey Glass Company, Jersey City, N.J., c. 1830–1840. L. 19.7 cm. Colorless lead glass, blown, cut. The Corning Museum of Glass (71.4.113).

36. **Pitcher**
Probably Union Flint Glass Company, Philadelphia, Pa., c. 1820–1840. H. 18.6 cm. Colorless (slightly yellowish) lead glass, blown, cut. The Corning Museum of Glass (71.4.78).

37. **Decanter or bottle**
Mount Vernon Glass Works, Mount Vernon, N.Y., c. 1825–1840. H. 20.9 cm. Transparent dark sage green nonlead glass, mold-blown. The Toledo Museum of Art (71.57, gift of Mrs. Harold G. Duckworth).

38. **Bowl**
Probably New England Glass Company, East Cambridge, or Boston and Sandwich Glass Company, Sandwich, Mass., c. 1818–1830. L. 26.5 cm. Colorless lead glass, mold-blown. The Corning Museum of Glass (75.4.34).

39. **Punch bowl**
Probably Boston and Sandwich Glass Company, Sandwich, Mass., c. 1825–1840. H. 15.3 cm. Colorless lead glass, mold-blown. The Toledo Museum of Art (59.61).

40. **Decanter and stopper**
Boston and Sandwich Glass Company, Sandwich, Mass., c. 1825–1840. OH. 22.9 cm. Transparent sapphire blue lead glass, mold-blown. The Toledo Museum of Art (17.247).

41. **Pitcher**
Boston and Sandwich Glass Company, Sandwich, Mass., c. 1825–1840. H. 16.8 cm. Colorless lead glass, mold-blown. The Corning Museum of Glass (55.4.204).

42. **George Washington and eagle flask**
Kensington Glass Works, Kensington, Philadelphia, Pa.,

c. 1826–1830. H. 17.8 cm. Transparent light green nonlead glass, mold-blown. Inscribed "Adams and Jefferson July 4 A.D. 1776 Kensington Glassworks, Philadelphia." The Corning Museum of Glass (60.4.14).

43. Columbia and eagle flask
Union Glass Works, Kensington, Philadelphia, Pa., c. 1826–1830. H. 19.0 cm. Transparent dark blue nonlead glass, mold-blown. The Corning Museum of Glass (60.4.123).

44. Louis Kossuth bottle
Probably Millford Glass Works, Millford, N.J., c. 1851–1855. H. 23.9 cm. Transparent light bluish green nonlead glass, mold-blown. Inscribed "U.S. STEAM FRIGATE/MISSISSIPPI/S. HUFFSEY." The base is inscribed "P. H. DOFLEIN/NTH. 5t St. 84/MOULD MAKER." The Toledo Museum of Art (17.438).

45. Railroad flask
Marlboro Street Glass Works, Keene, N.H., c. 1830–1840. H. 17.0 cm. Transparent amber nonlead glass, mold-blown, inscribed "Success to the Railroad." The Corning Museum of Glass (60.4.335).

46. Masonic and eagle flask
New England, c. 1818–1825. H. 19.2 cm. Transparent pale green lead glass, mold-blown. The Corning Museum of Glass (60.4.295).

47. Plate
New England, c. 1830–1835. D. 30.6 cm. Colorless lead glass, pressed in a "cut glass" pattern. The Corning Museum of Glass (68.4.115).

48. Dish
New England, c. 1830–1840. L. 30.8 cm. Colorless lead glass, pressed in a "peacock eye" pattern. The Corning Museum of Glass (68.4.425).

49. Casket with cover and tray
New England, c. 1835–1840. H. 13.3 cm. Opalescent deep blue lead glass, pressed in a pattern of Gothic arches. The Toledo Museum of Art (68.34).

50. Compote
New England, c. 1830–1845. H. 15.9 cm. Transparent amethyst lead glass, pressed in two parts, joined. The Corning Museum of Glass (68.4.219).

51. Tray
New England, c. 1830–1840. L. 24.0 cm. Colorless lead glass, pressed in the form of a shell with open loop handle. The Corning Museum of Glass (68.4.500).

52. Cup plate
Fort Pitt Glass Works, Pittsburgh, Pa., c. 1830–1845. D. 9.3 cm. Transparent dark blue lead glass, pressed eagle pattern, inscribed "FORT PITT." The Corning Museum of Glass (68.4.46).

53. Bar bottle
Probably Pittsburgh, Pa., c. 1855–1870. H. 25.5 cm. Transparent dark blue lead glass, mold-blown. The Toledo Museum of Art (65.5, gift of Mrs. Harold G. Duckworth).

54. Lamp
New England or Midwest, c. 1840–1860. H. 27.7 cm. Transparent deep amethyst lead glass, pressed in two parts, joined. The Corning Museum of Glass (68.4.457).

55. "Argus" pattern punch bowl
Bakewell, Pears & Company, Pittsburgh, Pa., c. 1850–1870. H. 30.5 cm. Colorless lead glass, pressed in two parts, joined. The Corning Museum of Glass (50.4.363).

56. "Pioneer" pattern covered butter dish
Gillinder & Sons, Philadelphia, Pa., c. 1876–1886. OH. 22.8 cm. Colorless nonlead glass, pressed. The Corning Museum of Glass (50.4.426).

57. Plate with portrait of President U. S. Grant
Probably Adams & Company, Pittsburgh, Pa., c. 1885. D. 26.6 cm. Transparent pale green nonlead glass, pressed. The Corning Museum of Glass (61.4.120).

58. Portrait bust of George Washington
Probably Bakewell, Pears & Company, Pittsburgh, Pa., c. 1876. H. 27.3 cm. Opalescent white nonlead glass, pressed, acid-etched matte surface. The Corning Museum of Glass (56.4.5).

59. Dolphin candlestick
New England, c. 1840–1860. H. 26.4 cm. Opalescent white and opaque light blue lead glass, pressed in two parts, joined. The Corning Museum of Glass (62.4.46).

60. Cane
Libbey Glass Company, Toledo, Ohio, c. 1902. OL. 187.0 cm. Colorless nonlead glass enclosing a flat strip of opalescent white with red and blue stripes on either side, twisted, drawn, and tooled to form a cane. The Toledo Museum of Art (68.61).

61. Compote
Probably New England Glass Company, East Cambridge, Mass., c. 1872–1876. H. 19.7 cm. Colorless lead glass, blown, cut. The Toledo Museum of Art (59.25).

62. Goblet
New England Glass Company, East Cambridge, Mass., engraved by Louis Vaupel, c. 1870–1875. H. 21.1 cm. Colorless lead glass overlaid with gold ruby, blown, cut, engraved. The Toledo Museum of Art (74.52).

63. Goblet
Probably New York City, possibly Christian Dorflinger or John Hoare, c. 1863–1875. H. 21.8 cm. Colorless lead glass, blown, cut, engraved. The Corning Museum of Glass (79.4.340, gift of The Ruth Bryan Strauss Memorial Foundation).

64. Punch bowl and cups
Libbey Glass Company, Toledo, Ohio, c. 1900. OH. (bowl) 34.1 cm., H. (cup) 8.6 cm. Colorless lead glass, blown, engraved. The engraved and polished (Rock Crystal style) bowl is marked (acid-etched) "Libbey." The Toledo Museum of Art (15.69, gift of Owens-Illinois, Inc.).

65. Five-piece place setting
Libbey Glass Company, Toledo, Ohio, 1904. H. (tallest) 16.5 cm. Colorless lead glass, blown, engraved, and polished (Rock Crystal style). The glasses are marked (acid-etched) "Libbey" on the upper surfaces of the feet. The Corning Museum of Glass (69.4.33, A,C, gift of Owens-Illinois, Inc., and The Toledo Museum of Art in honor of the Libbey Glass Company's 150th anniversary) and The Toledo Museum of Art (69.54, 69.84, 69.86).

66. "Russian" pattern Amberina pitcher
Probably New England Glass Works, East Cambridge, Mass.,

c. 1883–1888. H. 31.5 cm. Shaded red to yellow transparent lead glass, blown, cut. The Toledo Museum of Art (67.14, gift of Dorothy-Lee Jones).

67. "Russian" pattern salad set
Probably cut by T. G. Hawkes & Company, Corning, N.Y., c. 1882–1895; the blank probably made by Corning Glass Works, Corning, N.Y. D. 16.4 cm. Colorless lead glass, blown, cut. The Corning Museum of Glass (84.4.58, gift of Mr. and Mrs. John C. Huntington, Jr.).

68. "Venetian" pattern banquet lamp
Cut by T. G. Hawkes & Company, Corning, N.Y., c. 1890–1900; the blank made by Corning Glass Works, Corning, N.Y. H. 90.7 cm. Colorless lead glass, blown, cut; metal burner. The Corning Museum of Glass (82.4.9, gift of Helen Chambers in memory of Marvin W. Chambers).

69. Table
Libbey Glass Company, Toledo, Ohio, 1902. OH. 79.7 cm. Colorless lead glass, blown, cut. Marked (acid-etched) "Libbey" three times. The Toledo Museum of Art (51.1).

70. Vase
J. E. Haselbauer & Sons, Corning, N.Y., c. 1911–1920. H. 40.0 cm. Colorless lead glass, blown, cut, engraved; unmarked. The Corning Museum of Glass (78.4.5, gift of Mrs. C. L. Dencenburg).

71. Covered potpourri jar
H. P. Sinclaire & Company, blown at Dundee and engraved at Corning, N.Y., c. 1926. H. 20.4 cm. Colorless lead glass overlaid with transparent green, blown, engraved. Unmarked. The Corning Museum of Glass (84.4.165, gift of Mrs. Douglas Sinclaire).

72. Compote
Probably New England Glass Company, East Cambridge, or Boston Silver Glass Company, Boston, Mass., c. 1853–1875. H. 46.6 cm. Colorless lead glass, blown, engraved with mercury "silvering" inside; made in two parts, attached with a metal screw. The Corning Museum of Glass (68.4.1).

73. "Morgan Vase" and stand
Hobbs, Brockunier & Company, Wheeling, W.V., c. 1886–1891. OH. 25.5 cm. Shaded red to yellow transparent lead glass overlaid on opalescent white, mold-blown; the stand, transparent amber nonlead glass, pressed, acid-etched matte surface. The Corning Museum of Glass (50.4.328).

74. Champagne pitcher
Probably Boston and Sandwich Glass Company, Sandwich, or New England Glass Company, East Cambridge, Mass., c. 1870–1888. H. 28.0 cm. Colorless lead glass, blown, rolled in crushed glass to give an "ice glass" effect. The Corning Museum of Glass (74.4.115).

75. Royal Flemish vase
Mount Washington Glass Company, New Bedford, Mass., c. 1889–1895. H. 33.0 cm. Colorless lead glass, blown, enameled, raised gilding. The Corning Museum of Glass (63.4.138, gift of Fletcher Ford and Mrs. Sally Recker in memory of Lola Kincaid Ford).

76. Crown Milano cup and saucer
Mount Washington Glass Company, New Bedford, Mass., c. 1890–1895. H. (cup) 6.4 cm, D. (saucer) 12.7 cm. Translucent white lead glass, blown, acid-etched (matte) surface, relief-gilded,

marked with a gilded "CM" and a crown. The Corning Museum of Glass (79.4.342, bequest of Jerome Strauss).

77. Burmese lamp
Mount Washington Glass Company, New Bedford, Mass., c. 1885–1895. OH. 48.5 cm. Shaded pink to yellow translucent lead glass, blown, enameled; gilt-metal mounts. The Corning Museum of Glass (79.4.91, part gift of William E. Hammond).

78. Burmese vase
Mount Washington Glass Company, New Bedford, Mass., c. 1885–1895. H. 43.7 cm. Shaded pink to yellow translucent lead glass, blown, enameled. The Corning Museum of Glass (79.4.90, part gift of William E. Hammond).

79. Bellows bottle and stopper
Mount Washington Glass Company, New Bedford, Mass., blown by John Liddell, about 1885. OH. 50.0 cm. Transparent gold ruby overlaid with colorless lead glass, trailed opaque white threading drawn into loops, blown, applied decoration. The Toledo Museum of Art (54.12).

80. Paperweight mantel ornament
Attributed to Whitall Tatum Company, Millville, N.J., probably by Ralph Barber, about 1905–1912. H. 13.7 cm. Colorless, red, and green nonlead glass; "crimp" paperweight technique, lampworked elements. The Corning Museum of Glass (83.4.69, bequest of Clara S. Peck).

81. Punch bowl and cups
Northwood Glass Company, Wheeling, W.V., about 1910–1919. H. (bowl) 35.5 cm. Transparent amethyst glass, pressed, iridized; marked N in a circle on base. The Corning Museum of Glass (76.4.13, gift of Mr. and Mrs. Harold Ludeman).

82. Leaded glass landscape window
Tiffany Glass & Decorating Company or Tiffany Studios, Corona, Long Island, N.Y., c. 1900. H. 208.5 cm. Multicolored blown sheet glass, cut into elements and leaded together. The Corning Museum of Glass (81.4.168, gift of Seymour Koehl and Michael Cronin).

83. Laburnum lamp
Tiffany Studios, Corona, Long Island, N.Y., c. 1905. H. 65 cm. Multicolored blown sheet glass, cut into elements and leaded together; cast bronze base; the shade signed (impressed) "Tiffany Studios, New York 1539–5"; the base signed (impressed) "Tiffany Studios, New York 443." Lillian Nassau Ltd., New York City.

84. Flower-form vase
Tiffany Studios, Corona, Long Island, N.Y., c. 1900–1905. H. 32.3 cm. Colorless, transparent green, and translucent opalescent white lead glass, blown, trailed threading pulled into chevron patterns, iridized; signed on the base (engraved) "L.C.T. Y8281," with a fragmentary paper label. The Corning Museum of Glass (61.4.122).

85. Jack-in-the-Pulpit vase
Tiffany Studios, Corona, Long Island, N.Y., c. 1912. H. 47.6 cm. Transparent dark blue lead glass, blown, heavily iridized; signed (engraved) on the base "9557 G.-L. C. Tiffany-Favrile." The Corning Museum of Glass (62.4.61).

86. Vase
Tiffany Studios, Corona, Long Island, N.Y., c. 1906. H. 21.7 cm. Sealing-wax red glass with green and brownish amber aventurine

glass trailing, blown; signed on the bottom (engraved) "5557 M L. C. Tiffany Inc. Favrile Exhibition Piece." The Corning Museum of Glass (79.4.16).

87. Two stained-glass windows: *Beatrice* and *Dante*
William Willet and A. L. Willet, Willet Studios, Philadelphia, Pa., c. 1910–1920. OH. 119.0 cm. and 119.5 cm. Multicolored blown sheet glass, cut into elements and leaded together, enameled, stained; signed "W. Willet A. L. Willet." The Corning Museum of Glass (84.4.3, gift of Dr. Thomas H. English).

88. Vase
Steuben Glass Works, Corning, N.Y., c. 1910. H. 17.1 cm. Transparent amber lead glass, blown, heavily iridized; signed (engraved) "AURENE." The Corning Museum of Glass (75.4.113, gift of Corning Glass Works).

89. Water lamp
Steuben Division of Corning Glass Works, Corning, N.Y., c. 1920–1930. H. 39.3 cm. Transparent "Celeste Blue" lead glass, blown, pattern-molded "optic" ribbing, trailed; signed (engraved) "F. Carder." The Corning Museum of Glass (69.4.223, bequest of Gladys C. Welles).

90. Console set
H. P. Sinclaire & Company, blown in Bath and acid-etched and engraved in Corning, N.Y., c. 1920–1923. H. (tallest candlestick) 34.0 cm., D. (bowl) 45.1 cm. Opaque black and white nonlead glass, blown, acid-etched, engraved. The Corning Museum of Glass (85.4.4, gift of Mr. and Mrs. Morgan Sinclaire).

91. Vase
Frederick Carder, Corning Glass Works, Corning, N.Y., 1933–1934. H. 16.7 cm. Colorless lead glass with black flecks, cast using the lost wax method, cut and polished. Signed (engraved) "F. Carder." The Corning Museum of Glass (69.4.86, gift of Mr. and Mrs. Gillett Welles).

92. Gazelle bowl
Steuben Glass, Inc., Corning, N.Y., designed by Sidney Waugh, 1935. OH. 17.9 cm. Colorless lead glass, blown, cut, engraved; signed (diamond point) "Steuben." The Toledo Museum of Art (36.36).

93. The Valor Cup
Steuben Glass, Inc. Corning, N.Y., designed by John Monteith Gates, 1941. H. 39.8 cm. Colorless lead glass, blown, trailed, engraved; signed (diamond point) "Steuben." The Corning Museum of Glass (77.4.90, gift of the designer).

94. Decanter and cordial glass, *Modern America Series*
Libbey Glass Company, Toledo, Ohio, designed by Edwin W. Fuerst, 1940. H. (decanter) 29.0 cm., (cordial) 6.0 cm. Colorless lead glass, blown, cut; signed "Libbey." The Toledo Museum of Art (40.154, 40.168).

95. Pitcher
Viking Glass Company, New Martinsville, W.V., c. 1958. H. 34.4 cm. Transparent pale greenish gray nonlead glass, blown. The Corning Museum of Glass (61.4.162, gift of Viking Glass Company).

96. Uriel
Edris Eckhardt, Cleveland Heights, Ohio, 1968. H. 25.0 cm. Green and blue nonlead glass, cast (lost wax method); signed in the mold "Eckhardt 1968." The Corning Museum of Glass (68.4.28, gift of the artist).

97. Butterfly Finale
David White, Appalachian Center for Crafts, Smithville, Tenn., 1983. H. 30.1 cm. Colorless, transparent purple, and gray-white glass; blown, sandblasted, applied lampwork, acid etched; inscribed "David White/1983" and "Butterfly Finale." The Corning Museum of Glass (83.4.179).

98. Untitled
Harvey Littleton, Madison, Wis., 1965. H. 11.4 cm. Multicolored glass, silver oxide coloration and trailing, blown; inscribed "H. K. Littleton/1965." The Corning Museum of Glass (66.4.47).

99. Kisima
Steuben Glass, Inc., Corning, N.Y., designed by Donald Pollard (glass) and Bruce Moore (engraving), 1960. H. (with base) 15.5 cm. Colorless lead glass, cast, cut, engraved; signed (diamond point) "Steuben." The Corning Museum of Glass (82.4.57, bequest of Edwin J. Beinecke, Jr.).

100. Air sculpture
Dominick Labino, Grand Rapids, Ohio, 1969. H. 27.5 cm. Transparent light blue glass, air traps, internal gold veiling, hot-worked; inscribed "Labino/#3 1969." The Corning Museum of Glass (70.4.15).

101. Hand Form
Joel Philip Myers, Bloomington, Ill., 1972. H. 25.4 cm. Dark amber glass with silver nitrate striping, blown, manipulated while hot; inscribed "Joel Philip Myers 1972." The Corning Museum of Glass (73.4.71).

102. Fishbowl
Mark Peiser, Penland, N.C., 1972. H. 27.2 cm. Colorless, blue, green, and silver opalescent, yellow, orange, and blue glass; blown, applied decoration; inscribed "FISHBOWL #2 MARK PEISER 1972." The Toledo Museum of Art (72.91).

103. Acid Rain #2
Alan Klein, Boston, Mass., 1983. OW. 31.4 cm. Dark blue and green translucent glass, cast in a sand mold; inscribed "Alan Klein 83." The Corning Museum of Glass (84.4.8).

104. Ravenna Grand Jury/Masked Bandit
Henry Halem, Kent, Ohio, 1972. H. 28.1 cm. Opaque white glass, cast using the lost wax method. The Corning Museum of Glass (73.4.51).

105. Cicada necklace
Steuben Glass, Inc., Corning, N.Y., designed by Lloyd Atkins, 1978. L. (glass) 7.0 cm. Colorless lead glass, pressed; gold necklace; signed "Steuben." The Corning Museum of Glass (83.4.3).

106. Serie Fratelli Toso
Marvin Lipofsky, assisted by Gianni Toso, made in Murano, Italy, 1977–1978. H. 33.0 cm. Colorless, opaque white, red, and "black" amethyst glass; blown; inscribed "Lipofsky 78." The Corning Museum of Glass (79.4.15).

107. Spider's Nest
David R. Huchthausen, Madison, Wis., 1975. H. 46.9 cm. Black glass and tinted architectural glass, cast and hot-worked; cut plate glass, cemented and laminated. The Corning Museum of Glass (76.4.16, purchased with the aid of funds from the National Endowment for the Arts).

108. Teapot and Cozy
Richard Marquis, McKinleyville, Calif., 1973. H. 8.3 cm. Amethyst and opaque white glass, millefiori canes, blown; beaded leather cozy. The Corning Museum of Glass (75.4.29).

109. Space Cup No. 7
Michael Cohn, Berkeley, Calif., 1976. H. 10.3 cm. Blue, green, amber, and colorless glass; blown, cemented; inscribed "COHN 1976 S C #7." The Corning Museum of Glass (77.4.1).

110. A Cup with Appeal #2
Robert Levin, Burnsville, N.C., 1977. H. 21.7 cm. Opalescent, green, and dark blue ("black") glass, blown, sandblasted; signed "Robert Levin 1977." The Corning Museum of Glass (79.4.131, purchased with the aid of funds from the National Endowment for the Arts).

111. Untitled
Sonja Blomdahl, Seattle, Wash., 1986. H. 26.2 cm. Translucent yellow-pink, transparent aqua, and colorless glass; blown; inscribed "Sonja/SP 3986." The Corning Museum of Glass (86.4.94).

112. Purple Finch in the Snow
Roland "Rick" Ayotte, Nashua, N.H., 1982. D.7.0 cm. Colorless and polychrome glass, lampworked; signed "Ayotte 13/50 '82." The Corning Museum of Glass (82.4.4, gift of Theresa and Arthur Greenblatt and the artist).

113. Kally
Flora C. Mace and Joey Kirkpatrick, Pilchuck Glass Center, Stanwood, Wash., 1980. H. 20.4 cm. Gray and polychrome glass, blown, with metal wire and glass "drawing"; inscribed "Joey Kirkpatrick/Flora C. Mace/1980." The Corning Museum of Glass (84.4.20).

114. Pile Up
Harvey Littleton, Spruce Pine, N.C., 1979. OL. 80.3 cm. Optical glass bars, sagged; black plate glass, cut and polished; aluminum; inscribed "Harvey K. Littleton 1979 c." The Corning Museum of Glass (80.4.8, purchased with the aid of funds from the National Endowment for the Arts).

115. Indian Pipe
Paul J. Stankard, Mantua, N.J., 1987. H. 19.0 cm. Colorless and polychrome nonlead glass, lampworked; cut and laminated sides; inscribed "Paul J. Stankard C51 1987." The Corning Museum of Glass (87.4.50, gift of the Hon. and Mrs. Amory Houghton, by exchange).

116. Café
Dan Dailey, Amesbury, Mass., 1979. OH. 75.5 cm. Colorless, black, green, flesh, and red plate and tile glass; cut, polished, assembled; blown wineglass; inscribed "Dailey." The Corning Museum of Glass (80.4.63, purchased with the aid of funds from the National Endowment for the Arts).

117. Composition XXXI
Robert Kehlmann, Berkeley, Calif., 1976. H. 75.7 cm. Opalescent white, opaque white, and transparent blue, red, green, and amber glass; cut, leaded; signed "RK." The Corning Museum of Glass (79.4.11).

118. Baptismal Font
Kent F. Ipsen, Richmond, Va., 1978. D. 56.0 cm. Colorless glass with orange, amber, and opaque white inclusions; cast, acid-etched; inscribed "Ipsen/1978." The Corning Museum of Glass (79.4.8).

119. Untitled
Steven I. Weinberg, Providence, R.I., c. 1983. H. 6.0 cm. Colorless glass, cast; inscribed "Weinberg 831107." The Corning Museum of Glass (83.4.178).

120. Untitled
Peter Mollica, Oakland, Calif., 1977. OH. 82.2 cm. Transparent dark blue, translucent white, and colorless sheet glass; leaded, sandblasted; inscribed "Peter Mollica 1977." The Corning Museum of Glass (87.4.12, part gift of the artist).

121. Wisteria Trees PWV 079
Mark Peiser, Penland, N.C., 1978. H. 29.4 cm. Colorless and polychrome glass, blown, with lampworked and millefiori decoration; inscribed "MARK PEISER PWV 079—1978." The Corning Museum of Glass (79.4.135, purchased with the aid of funds from the National Endowment for the Arts).

122. Cityscape
Jay Musler, San Francisco, Calif., 1981. H. 23.2 cm. Colorless glass, blown, sandblasted, oil paint; inscribed "c 1981 Jay Musler CORCSG." The Corning Museum of Glass (82.4.8).

123. Fish Bowl
Doug Anderson, Mount Vernon, Ohio, 1982. H. 9.8 cm., D. 23.0 cm. Blue and green glass, cast, lost wax method, *pâte de verre*; inscribed "anderson/082682." The Corning Museum of Glass (83.4.2).

124. Macchia Sea Form Group
Dale Chihuly, Pilchuck School, Stanwood, Wash., 1982. W. (largest) 64.2 cm. Colorless, pink, and opaque white glass with amethyst and amber inclusions; blown; inscribed "Chihuly/1982." The Corning Museum of Glass (83.4.45, gift of Michael J. Bove III).

125. Banded Bronze
Thomas Patti, Savoy, Mass., 1976. H. 17.2 cm. Olive-amber, opaque white and gray, and colorless glass; laminated, blown, cut, polished; inscribed "Patti '76." The Corning Museum of Glass (79.4.134, purchased with the aid of funds from the National Endowment for the Arts).

126. Two Kinds of Animals Finding Their Equilibrium in Nature
Dudley F. Giberson, Jr., Warner, N.H., 1978. H. 20.1 cm. Amber glass with trailed and millefiori decoration, blown, fumed; signed "Giberson/78." The Corning Museum of Glass (79.4.124, purchased with the aid of funds from the National Endowment for the Arts).

127. Maelstrom
Michael Glancy, Pilchuck School, Stanwood, Wash., 1981. H. 13.3 cm. Deep red glass with blue and yellow striations, blown, sandblasted, polished, electroformed copper; inscribed "Michael M. Glancy 1981." The Corning Museum of Glass (85.4.93, gift of Joan and Bernard Chodorkoff).

128. Globe Form
Robert Clark Palusky, Deansboro, N.Y., 1986. H. 35.4 cm. Translucent opal and colorless glass, smoked flat glass; blown, ground, sandblasted, painted, laminated sheet glass; inscribed "Robert Palusky/1986." The Corning Museum of Glass (86.4.203, gift of the artist).

129. Untitled, African Dream Series
Mary Ann "Toots" Zynsky, made in Amsterdam, The Netherlands, 1983. H. 12.2 cm. Colorless (slight blue-gray tint) glass, pulled, fused and slumped rods; inscribed "Z." The Corning Museum of Glass (84.4.109).

130. Untitled
Richard Meitner, made in Amsterdam, The Netherlands, 1984. H. 30.7 cm. Colorless glass, blown, enameled; inscribed "R. Meitner 84." The Corning Museum of Glass (84.3.47).

131. #75–64 Contrapuntal Series
William Carlson, Champaign, Ill., 1985. OH. 34.0 cm. Colorless, black, blue. and gray glass; cast, cut, assembled; inscribed "William Carlson 1985 ©." The Corning Museum of Glass (85.4.18).

132. 2011 CSDV and DV 1504
James R. Harmon, Normal, Ill., 1977. H. 26.8 and 17.9 cm. Colorless glass with colored inclusions, blown, joined while hot, fumed; inscribed "2011 CSDV James R. Harmon 1977" and "DV 1504/James R. Harmon/1977." The Corning Museum of Glass (79.4.125 and 79.4.126, purchased with the aid of funds from the National Endowment for the Arts).

133. Spoke
Karla Trinkley, Boyertown, Pa., 1986. H. 31.0 cm. Deep blue and aqua glass, cast (lost wax method), painted. The Corning Museum of Glass (86.4.97).

134. New York, New York
Steuben Glass, Inc., Corning, N.Y., designed by Paul Schulze, 1984.

H. 43.2 cm., Colorless lead glass, cast, cut, polished, engraved; signed (diamond point) "Steuben." The Corning Museum of Glass (87.4.2, anonymous gift.)

135. Japanese Headdress
James van Deurzen, Creative Glass Center of America, Millville, N.J., 1984. OH. 58.7 cm. Colorless and polychrome glass, blown in sections, cut, sandblasted, fused; inscribed "Van Deurzen/ #2021/'84." The Corning Museum of Glass (85.4.44).

136. Totem
Mark Abildgaard, Creative Glass Center of America, Millville, N.J., 1985. H. 102.0 cm. Colorless glass with red and yellow cane decoration, cast in a sand mold, colored glass inclusions; inscribed "Mark Abildgaard 1985." The Corning Museum of Glass (87.4.5).

137. Swimmer
Stephen Dale Edwards, Kirkland, Wash., 1983. H. 32.8 cm. Colorless and transparent amber glass, blown, "Graal" technique, cut, kiln-formed; inscribed "Stephen Dale Edwards '83." The Corning Museum of Glass (83.4.29).

138. Untitled
William Morris, Pilchuck School, Stanwood, Wash., 1982. H. 76.5 cm. Colorless and polychrome glass, mold-blown; inscribed "William Morris 1982" The Corning Museum of Glass (82.4.20).

139. Untitled
Howard Ben Tré, Providence, R.I., 1982. H. 38.5 cm. Greenish translucent glass, cast in a sand mold; applied copper sheeting and oxide. The Toledo Museum of Art (86.75).

Bibliography

Corning Museum of Glass. *Glass 1959: A Special Exhibition of Contemporary Glass*. Corning, N.Y.: the Museum, 1959.

———. *New Glass, A Worldwide Survey*. Exhibition, April 26–Oct. 1, 1979. Corning, N.Y.: the Museum, 1979.

———. *New Glass Review 1–10*. Corning, N.Y.: the Museum, 1980–1987.

Frantz, Susanne K. *Contemporary Glass: A World Survey from The Corning Museum of Glass*. New York: Harry N. Abrams, 1989.

Gardner, Paul V. *Frederick Carder: Portrait of a Glassmaker*. Corning, N.Y.: the Museum, 1985.

———. *The Glass of Frederick Carder*. New York: Crown Publishers, 1971.

Heacock, William. *The Encyclopedia of Victorian Colored Pattern Glass, Books 1–9*. Marietta, Ohio: Antique Publications, 1974–1988.

Huntington Galleries. *New American Glass: Focus [1]–2 West Virginia*. Huntington, W.V.: the Museum, 1976, 1986.

Innes, Lowell. *Pittsburgh Glass 1797–1893, A History and a Guide for Collectors*. Boston: Houghton Mifflin, 1976.

Lanmon, Dwight P., and Arlene M. Palmer. "John Frederick Amelung and the New Bremen Glassmanufactory," *Journal of Glass Studies* 18 (1976). Corning, N.Y.: the Museum, 1976.

Leigh Yawkey Woodson Art Museum. *Americans in Glass*, [1–3]. Wasau, Wis., the Museum, 1979, 1981, 1984.

Madigan, Mary Jean. *Steuben Glass: An American Tradition in Crystal*. New York: Harry N. Abrams, 1982.

McKean, Hugh F. *The "Lost" Treasures of Louis Comfort Tiffany*. New York: Doubleday & Company, 1980.

McKearin, George S. and Helen. *American Glass*. New York: Crown Publishers, 1948. 23rd printing.

———. *Two Hundred Years of American Blown Glass*. Garden City, N.Y.: Doubleday, 1950.

McKearin, Helen, and Kenneth M. Wilson. *American Bottles and Flasks and Their Ancestry*. New York: Crown Publishers, 1978.

Melvin, Jean S. *American Glass Paperweights and Their Makers*. Rev. ed. New York: Thomas Nelson, 1970.

Peterson, Arthur G. *400 Trademarks on Glass, with Alphabetical Index*. Rev. ed. Stamford, Conn.: JO-D Books, 1985.

Revi, Albert C. *American Art Nouveau Glass*. Camden, N.J.: Thomas Nelson and Sons, 1968.

Spillman, Jane Shadel. *American and European Pressed Glass in the Corning Museum of Glass*. Corning, N.Y.: the Museum, 1981. Corning Museum of Glass Catalog Series.

———. *Glassmaking, America's First Industry*. Corning, N.Y.: the Museum, 1976.

Swan, Martha Louise. *American Cut and Engraved Glass of the Brilliant Period in Historical Perspective*. Illinois: Wallace-Homestead Book Company, 1986.

Wilson, Kenneth M. *New England Glass and Glassmaking*. New York: Thomas Y. Crowell Company, 1972.

Index